ENZO ANGELUCCI   PAOLO MATRICARDI

COMBAT AIRCRAFT
OF WORLD WAR II
1941-1942

Illustrations by Pierluigi Pinto

a Salamander book

Published by Salamander Books Limited
LONDON • NEW YORK

Created by Adriano Zannino
Editorial assistant Serenella Genoese Zerbi
Editor: Maria Luisa Ficarra
Translated from the Italian by Ruth Taylor

Consultant for color plate Bruno Benvenuti

Published by Salamander Books Ltd,
52 Bedford Row,
London WC1R 4LR
United Kingdom

ISBN 0 86101 415 4

Distributed in the UK by
Hodder & Stoughton Services,
P.O. Box 6,
Mill Road,
Dunton Green,
Sevenoaks,
Kent TN3 2XX

Printed in Italy by SAGDOS S.p.A., Milan

All correspondence concerning the contents of
this volume should be addressed to
Salamander Books Ltd.

THE GREAT POTENTIAL OF NAVAL AVIATION

Monday, November 14, 1910. Eugene Ely, a young "heavier-than-air" enthusiast, takes off in a Curtiss biplane from an 82-foot long (25 m) wooden platform installed on board the American cruiser *Birmingham*, anchored in Hampton Road bay, Virginia. This was the first time such an endeavor had been attempted, but the flight took place without any problems, and the pilot landed at Willoughby Spit nearby. Another success was achieved two months later, on January 18, 1911, when Ely, once again at the controls of a Curtiss biplane, left San Francisco and flew some 12 miles (20 km) over the sea, landing on the platform of the cruiser *Pennsylvania*, which lay at anchor, before taking off again for Selfridge Field less than an hour later.

At that time, the airplane was taking the first steps in the difficult terrain of official public opinion, and these tests were carried out in a climate of general skepticism on the part of the U.S.Navy. Nevertheless, the result was uncontestable: Glenn Hammond Curtiss with his biplane and Eugene Ely with his courage proved without a shadow of doubt that it was possible to exploit the great potential of the aircraft also on board a warship. Many years were to pass after these two historic dates before this new, revolutionary military concept was entirely accepted and put into practice (the use of a land aircraft from a «real» aircraft carrier began in 1917, following the conversion of the British cruiser *Furious*), although the seed had already been sown. Naval aviation was not immediately synonymous with carrier-based aviation, but the process was gradual, and the first aircraft to make their mark were those in which the adaptation to the sea seemed more "natural": seaplanes.

The challenge of conquering the sky by taking off not only from land but also from water had been strongly felt by the pioneers of "heavier-than-air" flight. The first flight of this kind had been carried out by Gabriel Voisin on the Seine, in Paris, on June 6, 1905. This had not involved an engine-driven aircraft, but simply a glider that had succeeded in taking off from the surface of the river while being towed by a motorboat. Five years later, on March 28, 1910, success was achieved thanks to the tenacity of another Frenchman, Henry Fabre, who had tested his Hydravion, the first seaplane in history, at Martigues, near Marseilles. It was an awkward and fragile monoplane with a driving propeller powered by a 50 hp Gnome rotary engine and fitted with floats.

This was still one of the earliest steps, but Fabre's experiences were followed up in the United States by Glenn Hammond Curtiss, to whom goes the merit for having improved upon them in a definitive manner. On January 26, 1911, at San Diego, California, Curtiss successfully tested his seaplane, which was derived from the famous Golden Bug biplane, and an entire series of other models was created from this initial aircraft, rapidly focusing worldwide attention on the American manufacturer. The Curtiss seaplane proved to be so effective that it aroused great interest in the U.S.Navy, which bought it in July, designating it A.1. The experiment that led to this historic decision was a flight carried out by Curtiss on February 17, 1911, during which his aircraft took off from a base along the coast and reached the cruiser *Pennsylvania*, anchored off San Diego. The A.1 seaplane, as well as going down in history as the first "heavier-than-air" in the American navy, also had the merit of qualifying the first American naval pilot, Lieutenant Theodore G. Ellyson. Moreover, Ellyson carried out a series of experiments with the aircraft aimed at improving the techniques of catapult launching.

It was World War I that revealed the new possibilities offered by the aircraft in naval warfare and stimulated both the use of seaplanes and the development of new aircraft carriers by the major powers in a decisive way. As far as the latter were concerned, the British were the first to realize the potential of carrier-based aviation and to transform it into reality: in 1917, on the basis of a project by Admiral Jack Fisher, the cruiser *Furious* was provided with a real flight deck, with elastic arresting cables and safety barriers, and altered in such a way as to be able to carry and render operative 17-18 aircraft. In fact, on July 19, 1918, it was from this very ship that the first offensive operation in history to be launched from an aircraft carrier against targets on land took place: eight Sopwith Camel biplanes bombed a German dirigible base, destroying two airships. The *Furious* was soon followed by the *Argus* and the *Eagle*, the first aircraft carrier with superstructures grouped in the characteristic asymmetrical "island" configuration, in order to leave the largest amount of space possible for the flight deck.

The role of the aircraft carrier was accepted definitively in the years following the end of the Great War and was formally sanctioned by the Washington Naval Conference of 1921, during which constraints on their construction were imposed: for the United States and Great Britain the total displacement of these vessels was not to exceed 135,000 tons; for Japan, 91,000 tons; for Italy and France 60,000 tons.

At the time, Great Britain already had four ships of this type, the United States was about to put the *Langley* (derived from a coal ship) into service, and Japan was preparing the *Shoho*. In fact, during the next few years, a veritable race broke out between these countries, placing them in the vanguard at an international level: the *Lexington* and the *Saratoga* were built by the United States; the *Akagi* and the *Kaga*, by Japan; the *Ark Royal*, the four ships of the *Illustrious* series, the *Implacable* and *Indefatigable* were constructed by Great Britain.

This marked the beginning of a confrontation that was to continue until it erupted in the direct challenge of the fresh conflict, and it developed at the same time not only in the field of naval construction, but also in that of strict aeronautics with manufacturers concentrating ever increasing interest and resources in the category of carrier-based combat planes which, from machines sometimes adapted from those used on land and generally inferior to them, became increasingly specialized, designed and built bearing in mind the particular structural characteristics and the performance necessary for this specific use. In many cases (the example of the Japanese Mitsubishi A6M Reisen, the famous Zero, which became the very symbol of Japanese air power in the Pacific, is valid for all) "naval" aircraft proved to be far superior to their land counterparts.

The conflict in the Pacific clearly showed just how much carrier-based aviation had changed the scenario of war on the sea. From Pearl Harbor onward the aircraft carriers played decisive roles, revolutionizing the traditional concepts of naval battle and they eventually replaced the battleships in the role of the fleet's capital ships. Tactical and strategical targets were no longer hit by direct cannon shots, but through the use of aircraft with a combat range ten times greater than that of simple ballistic contact. The aircraft consequently became the true protagonist. From the battle of the Coral Sea in May 1942 (the first naval encounter in which the outcome was determined exclusively by aviation) to Midway and all subsequent operations, naval power could no longer be separated from that of the aircraft.

This was a lesson that was learnt by all, winners and losers, although some of the powers at war (such as Germany or Italy) never had the occasion to make use of it. In fact, in Germany the only aircraft carrier to be built was the *Graf Zeppelin*, which never went into service, although launched in 1938. In Italy, it was not until July 1941, following defeat in the naval battle of Cape Matapan, that it was decided to construct an aircraft carrier: the *Aquila*. This was to have been followed by a second (the *Sparviero*), but the events of the war made these desperate attempts useless. As for France, the *Béarn* fell victim to the armistice.

1942

January 2	The Japanese take Manila.
February 15	Singapore surrenders to the Japanese: 70,000 British, Australian, and Indian troops are taken prisoner.
February 27	Naval battle in the Java Sea between an Allied squadron and the invading Japanese fleet. The encounter ended in victory for the Japanese.
March 7	The Japanese invasion of Java is almost complete.
March 17	General Douglas MacArthur assumes supreme command of the Allied forces in the Southwest Pacific. Three days later, General Wainwright is placed in command of all the American forces in the Philippines.
April 9	The resistance of the defenders of Bataan falls: following the unconditional surrender, 76,000 men are taken prisoner by the Japanese.
April 18	American B-25 Mitchells, that took off from the aircraft carrier *Hornet*, carry out a raid on Tokyo.
May 8	The air-sea battle in the Coral Sea comes to an end. This was the first air-sea encounter in history to be fought exclusively by aircraft, without the opposing fleets coming into direct contact. The result favored the Americans.
May 30-31	More than 1,000 British bombers carry out a massive raid on Cologne.
June 3	The United States declares war on Rumania, Bulgaria and Hungary.
June 4-7	Air-sea battle of Midway. This marked the turning point in the war in the Pacific: the balance tipped in favor of the American troops, who gradually consolidated their supremacy over their adversary.
July 2	The fortress of Sevastopol falls: the German attack had commenced on June 7.
July 8	Admiral Nimitz issues his plan of action: the American troops were to take Santa Cruz, as well as Tulagi and Guadalcanal in the Solomon Islands.
August 8	Air-sea battle of Savo Island. A Japanese squadron takes by surprise the Allied fleet protecting troopships destined for the invasion of the Solomon Islands, inflicting serious damage in the course of the nightime encounter.
November 8	American troops land in Morocco and Algeria as part of Operation Torch. The aim of this operation, agreed by Churchill and Roosevelt on July 25, was to open up a new front in northwest Africa.

LOCKHEED P-38G

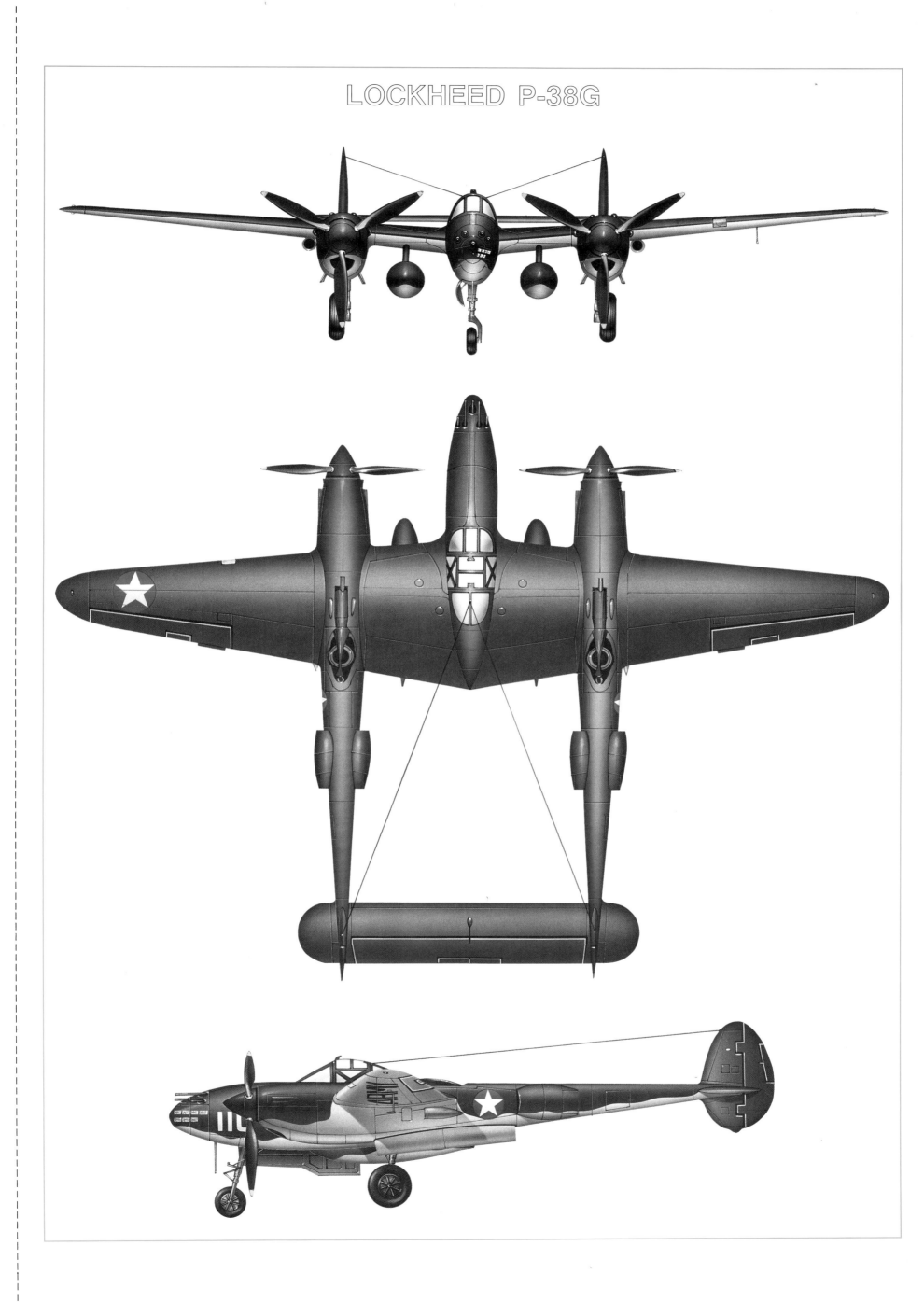

Lockheed's first military aircraft to go into production was also one of the most famous and effective fighters of World War II. Between 1940 and 1945 almost 10,000 P-38 Lightnings were built. The aircraft was powerful and versatile, as well as being very unusual: it was the first two-engine interceptor to go into service in the USAAC; the first American fighter to surpass 400 mph (644 km/h); and the first production series aircraft to have double tail fins. The Lightning had a long and extensive career, during which it was used on practically all fronts in a great variety of roles, thus revealing the great potential of the original project. In fact, as well as serving as an interceptor, it was also used for photographic reconnaissance missions, as a fighter-bomber and as a night fighter. Christened *Der Gabelschwanz Teufel* ("The Devil with the Cleft Tail") by the Germans and "Two fighters, one pilot" by the Japanese, the P-38 was also the first USAAF fighter to shoot down one of the Luftwaffe's planes as well as being that which destroyed more Japanese aircraft than any other. The Lightning was also the aircraft used by the leading American aces in the conflict: Major Richard I. Bong (40 aircraft shot down), Major Thomas B. McGuire (38) and Colonel H. McDonald (27). Bong in fact shot down all his adversaries while flying a P-38, between December 12, 1942, and December 17, 1944. Among the numerous war missions in which the Lockheed fighter played a major role, one of the most memorable occurred on April 18, 1943, when a Lightning intercepted and shot down the two-engine G4M carrying Admiral Isoroku Yamamoto, commander-in-chief of the Japanese fleet, and the man who had planned the attack on Pearl Harbor.

The specifications that gave rise to the P-38 were issued by the technical authorities of the U.S.Army Air Corps in 1937. They called for a high-altitude interceptor capable of reaching 360 mph (580 km/h) at 20,000 feet (6,100 m) and 290 mph (467 km/h) at sea level. It was also to be capable of reaching its optimum ceiling in six minutes. These characteristics were far to be easy to satisfy in a monoplane of traditional configuration, but Lockheed's chief designers, Hall L. Hibbard and Clarence L. "Kelly" Johnson, were not to be discouraged, and they examined six possible solutions before presenting their Model 22. This was a middle wing two-engine aircraft with double tail beams (this solution was necessary in order to house the engines and their superchargers), central pod for the pilot and armament, double vertical tail units linked by a single horizontal plane, and a completely retractable tricycle forward landing gear. The project proved to be a success, and on June 23, 1937, a prototype was ordered. This took to the air on January 27, 1939, and before official evaluations, the USAAC decided to use it in an attempt at breaking the speed record for crossing the United States from coast to coast. The flight took place on February 11: from March Field in California to Mitchell Field, New York, in seven hours 43 minutes, including two stops for refueling. The aircraft crashed when landing due to a fault in one of the engines, but its effectiveness as a combat plane had been proved sensationally. On April 27, an order was placed for 13 preseries YP-38s, followed immediately after by the first contracts for production-series aircraft.

Following the construction of the first 29 P-38s, which were substantially the same as the prototype, 36 P-38Ds (with modifications to the systems on board) came off the assembly lines, together with 210 P-38Es (the first major production version, with heavier armament and in service from November 1941). At the same time a variant destined for export to Great Britain was prepared. In fact the British, who were in desperate need of fighters, had ordered no fewer than 667 P-38s in March 1940. However, the engines of these aircraft were not provided with superchargers, and their performance was decidedly inferior. They were therefore rejected by the RAF: 147 of the 150 ordered initially were completed in the United States as the P-38F. This variant (which went into production early in 1942 and was operative by March) was the first to see combat, initially in Europe toward the middle of the year and then in North Africa in November. It had more powerful engines and wing racks for bombs or supplementary fuel tanks. A total of 527 was built in all. These were followed by 1082 P-38Gs.

A P-38 in flight with one engine immobile.

A Lockheed F-5, the photo reconnaissance version of the P-38G in which the armament was replaced by photographic equipment. This aircraft (2364) was one of the first American planes to operate from the airports on the island of Malta, piloted by Lt. Berry.

color plate

Lockheed P-38G piloted by Captain Thomas G. Lanphier Jr. 339th Fighter Squadron U.S. Air Force. This aircraft took part in the shooting down of the plane carrying Admiral Yamamoto, the commander-in-chief of the Japanese Imperial Navy Combined Fleet on April 18, 1943

Aircraft:	Lockheed P-38F
Nation:	USA
Manufacturer:	Lockheed Aircraft Corp.
Type:	Fighter
Year:	1942
Engine:	2 Allison V-1710-49, 12-cylinder V, liquid-cooled, 1,385 hp each
Wingspan:	52 ft 1 in (15.84 m)
Length:	37 ft 10 in (11.53 m)
Height:	12 ft 10 in (3.91 m)
Weight:	20,000 lb (9,065 kg) loaded
Maximum speed:	395 mph (636 km/h) at 25,000 ft (7,620 m)
Ceiling:	39,000 ft (11,880 m)
Range:	425 miles (684 km)
Armament:	1 × 20 mm cannon; 4 machine guns; 2,002 lb (907 kg) of bombs
Crew:	1

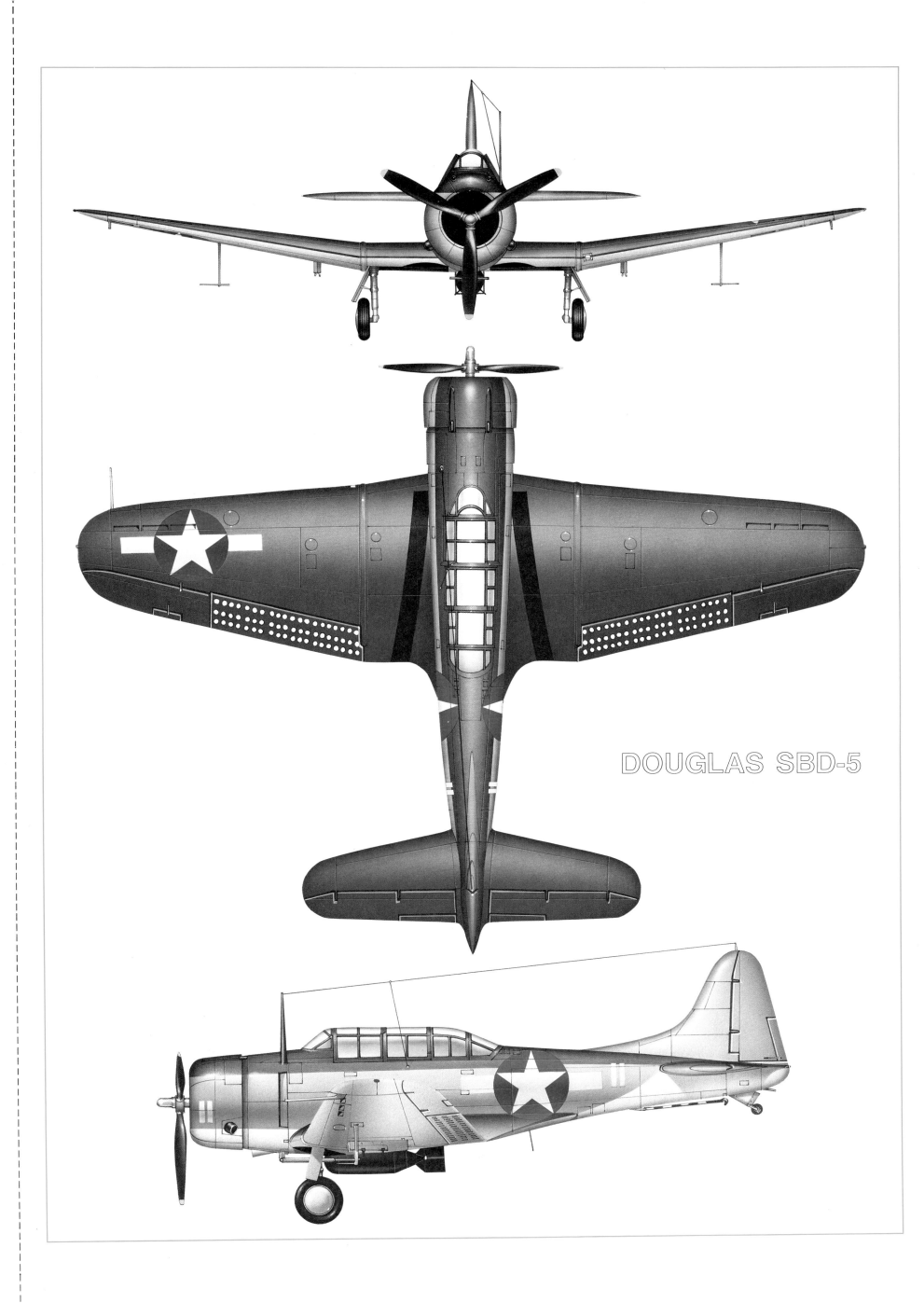

DOUGLAS SBD-5

Although conceived in 1938, the Douglas SBD Dauntless has gone down in history as the best dive-bomber built by the American aeronautical industry during World War II. A total of 5,936 was built in all, and this tough monoplane remained in front-line service in the units of the U.S.Navy and the U.S.Marine Corps until the end of 1944, when it was relegated to secondary roles. However, many SBDs survived the conflict and remained in service for several years after the war had ended. In the course of its long and extensive career, the Dauntless' greatest moment of glory occurred during the air-sea battles that took place in 1942, marking the turning point in the war in the Pacific. On May 7, during the Battle of the Coral Sea, SBDs based on the aircraft carriers *Yorktown* and *Lexington* sank the Japanese carrier *Shoho*. At Midway a month later, on June 4, the *Akagi*, the *Kaga*, and the *Soryu* were also sunk, while the *Hiryu* was seriously damaged.

The project for the Dauntless was directly derived from that of the Northrop BT-1, which had started to go into service in the U.S.Navy in the spring of 1938. In fact, at that time, the Northrop Corporation was about to become a subsidiary of the Douglas Company, and the new aircraft was given the designation characteristic of the latter company. Although the prototype was very similar to its direct predecessor, it was much more advanced, and flight tests immediately revealed its excellent qualities. The aircraft was a low-wing two-seater monoplane with retractable landing gear. It was all-metal, with the exception of the steering areas, which were fabric-covered, and was provided with an arrester hook. It was powered initially by a 1,000 hp Wright XR-1820-32 Cyclone radial engine.

In April 1939 the first orders were placed for 57 SBD-1s and 87 SBD-2s (the latter had a greater fuel capacity and modified armament) by the U.S.Marine Corps and the U.S.Navy respectively. These Dauntlesses went into service beginning at the end of 1940. However, in March of the following year, they were replaced by the first aircraft of the SBD-3 version, which had strengthened and improved armament as well as more protection.

When the war against Japan broke out, these aircraft were sent to equip the bomber units based on the aircraft carriers *Lexington*, *Enterprise*, *Yorktown* and *Saratoga*. Beginning in 1942 production was heavily increased, and following the construction of 584 SBD-3s and 780 SBD-4s (which differed only in that their electrical system was 24 volts instead of 12), the SBD-5 appeared. This was the major variant and was characterized by the adoption of a 1,217 hp Wright engine, and by improvements to the

armament and systems on board. After the assembly lines had completed 2,409 SBD-5s, the final SBD-6 version appeared. This was fitted with a 1,350 hp engine and had a greater fuel capacity. Production came to an end in July 1944.

However, the Dauntless' career was not limited solely to its service in the units of the U.S. Navy and the U.S.Marine Corps. In 1940, impressed by the great successes scored in Europe by the German Junkers Ju.87 Stuka dive-bomber, the U.S.Army Air Corps realized that it did not have a similar weapon at its disposal and hurriedly ordered 78 SBD-3s without equipment for naval use from Douglas. This initial order was followed by another for 90 aircraft, which were redesignated A-24. In November 1941, 52 of these aircraft were sent to the Philippines. However, following the surprise attack on Pearl Harbor, they were transferred to Australia and subsequently to the Dutch Indies. It was in this theater of operations that the A-24s first saw combat, but strangely their performance was not considered satisfactory. Nevertheless, orders were placed for a further 170 A-24As (the equivalent of the SBD-4) and 615 A-24Bs (similar to the SBD-5). Most of these aircraft were used for training duty.

---

color plate

Douglas SBD-5 V.C.40 U.S.Navy Air Force - Torokina, Bougainville, New Guinea, April 1944

Aircraft:	Douglas SBD-3
Nation:	USA
Manufacturer:	Douglas Aircraft Co.
Type:	Bomber
Year:	1941
Engine:	Wright R-1820-52 Cyclone, 9-cylinder radial, air-cooled, 1,000 hp
Wingspan:	41 ft 6 in (12.65 m)
Length:	32 ft 8 in (9.96 m)
Height:	13 ft 7 in (4.14 m)
Weight:	10,400 lb (4,717 kg) loaded
Maximum speed:	250 mph (402 km/h)
Ceiling:	27,100 ft (8,260 m)
Range:	1,345 miles (2,164 km)
Armament:	4 machine guns; 1,200 lb (544 kg) of bombs
Crew:	2

An example of the Douglas SBD-3, redesignated A-24 in flight with the defensive position on the back open.

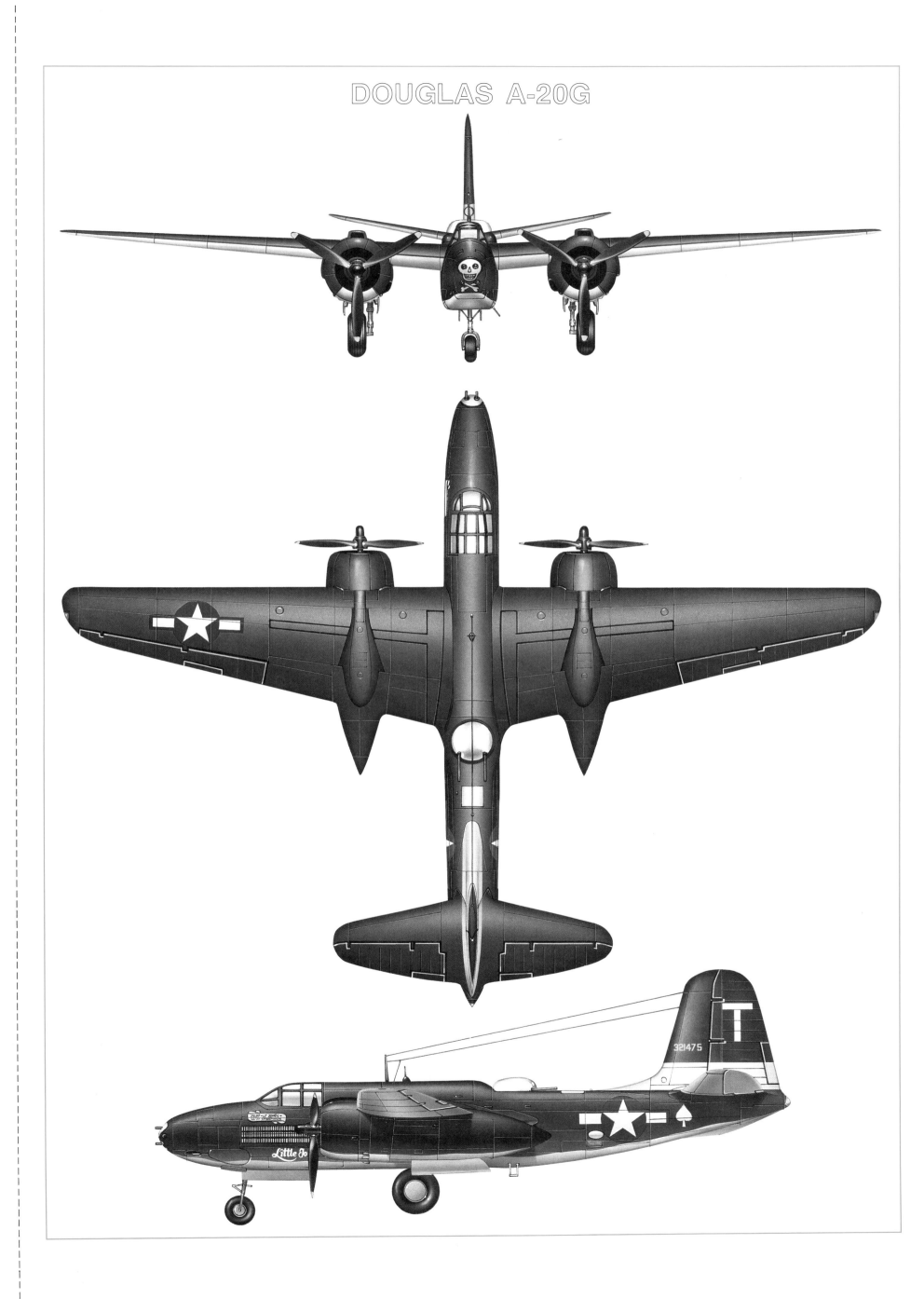

In production from 1939 to 1944, a total of 7,385 of the light, two-engine Douglas was built in numerous versions, and they constituted one of the most prolific and versatile families of fighting aircraft built by the American aeronautical industry during the war. These aircraft were known by various names and designations in the course of their long and extensive operative career. The best known of these were DB-7 in France (the first nation to place an order for them, in 1938, in the wake of the *Armée de l'Air*'s urgent need for rearmament); Boston and Havoc in Great Britain; and A-20, P-70, A-3 in the United States. Bomber, fighter, ground attack, night fighter, reconnaissance: the two-engine Douglas operated in all of these roles and on all fronts from the first day of the conflict to the last. Among the countries that adopted the aircraft, prime position was held by the Soviet Union, which received almost half of the entire production, a total of 3,215 aircraft.

The project originated in 1936. At that time, although no official specifications had been issued, Douglas was considering the development of a high-performance modern tactical bomber to offer to the USAAC. The project, initially designated Model 7A and entrusted to the chief designer, Ed Heinemann, assumed its definitive form in 1938, and its maiden flight took place on October 26. It was an elegant, all-metal middle high-wind two-engine aircraft with retractable tricycle forward landing gear and was powered by a pair of 1,115 hp Pratt & Whitney R-1830 Twin Wasp radial engines. An unusual feature was the interchangeable formula foreseen for the tip of the nose in order to facilitate the production of the bomber and ground-attack versions.

Despite the plane's promising performance, the U.S.Army Air Corps did not show an immediate interest in the new aircraft, and Douglas began to search for a foreign buyer. The first order, placed by France, was not long in coming and was for an initial lot of 105 aircraft. Redesignated DB-7 and substantially modified in order to make it more suited to the operative needs of the war in Europe, the first production series aircraft took to the air on August 17, 1939. The *Armée de l'Air* subsequently placed orders for a total of 260 DB-7s and almost 700 DB-7As (with improvements to the equipment and armament and provided with more powerful engines). To these was added a small order from Belgium for 16 aircraft. However, the course of the war drastically reduced the deliveries to the *Armée de l'Air* and most of the aircraft ordered were subsequently sent to Great Britain. These planes (which the RAF designated Boston and Havoc, the former

A night fighter variant of the Havoc, equipped with radar and designated P-70.

being the bomber version and the latter the night-fighter version) became operative toward the end of 1940.

In the meantime, the USAAC had begun to show an interest. An initial contract had been signed in May 1939, immediately after the French one, and concerned 63 aircraft designated A-20. Provided with R-2600 series Wright engines, three of them were transformed into prototypes for photographic reconnaissance (XF-3) and one into the prototype of a night fighter (XP-70). The remaining 59 (P-70A-1) were the first production series with this specialization. Later, the first bomber variants, the A-20A and A-20B, also appeared (with 143 and 999 being built respectively) with improvements above all to the engines. Production was standardized with the next version, the A-20C (known as the Boston Mk.III in the RAF). In May 1942, these aircraft were the first to see combat bearing American insignia in Europe.

In the same year the major production variant appeared. This was the A-20G and was destined exclusively for the USAAF and the Soviet air force, a total of 2,850 being built in all. Characterized by the adoption of a solid nose with heavy offensive armament, this aircraft proved to be particularly effective in ground attack and scored some great successes, especially on the Pacific front. The next version, the A-20H, was very similar but was provided with more powerful engines; 412 were built. The final variants, the J and K, were derived from this and the previous variant, but they marked a return to the glazed-in nose and the role of traditional bomber. These series (of which 450 and 413 were built respectively) served in the RAF as Boston Mk.IVs and Mk.Vs.

A Douglas A-20G in flight; the aircraft's armament is concentrated in the nose.

color plate
Douglas A-20G Havoc 389th Bomber Squadron 312th Bomber Group 5th Air Force U.S.Army Air Force-Florida Blanca Airfield, Luzon, the Philippines, January 1945

Aircraft: Douglas A-20G	
Nation: USA	
Manufacturer: Douglas Aircraft Co.	
Type: Bomber	
Year: 1942	
Engine: 2 Wright R-2600-23 Cyclone, 14-cylinder radial, air-cooled, 1,622 hp each	
Wingspan: 61 ft 4 in (18.69 m)	
Length: 48 ft (14.63 m)	
Height: 17.17 ft 7 in (5.63 m)	
Weight: 27,200 lb (12,338 kg) loaded	
Maximum speed: 339 mph (545 km/h) at 12,400 ft (3,780 m)	
Ceiling: 25,065 ft (7,620 m)	
Range: 1,090 miles (1,750 km)	
Armament: 9 machine guns; 4,004 lb (1,814 kg) of bombs	
Crew: 3	

THE UNITED STATES OF AMERICA

"Perhaps we have only awoke a giant who was sleeping". This was the comment made by the artificer of Pearl Harbor, Admiral Isoroku Yamamoto, on the speech that the American President Franklin D. Roosevelt delivered to Congress on December 8, 1941, a few hours after the Japanese attack. Rarely has a forecast been more accurate. What is still known today in the history of the United States as the "day of infamy" was also the beginning of a reaction that was to continue in a powerful and unhaltable fashion for the rest of the conflict.

Until then the "sleeping giant" had considered the war as an event that concerned it only from a distance, separated as it was by two oceans from the potential adversaries in Europe and in Asia. Direct involvement, in its brutal reality, was a veritable blow rather than an awakening. With the entry of the United States into the war, the entire energy of the nation was activated to the maximum. The most advanced industrial network in the world, until then involved in the conflict more or less to satisfy the requests of the European Allies who had already been fighting against the Third Reich for two years, utilized its resources to the full, assigning them entirely to the defense and needs of the country.

Nevertheless, the earliest months of the war were still marked by the crushing supremacy of Japan, both from a quantitative and a qualitative point of view, compared to the weak and unorganized Allied forces. From Pearl Harbor until the spring of 1942, the forces of the Rising Sun managed to achieve all the objectives that had been set, spreading across Malaysia, Burma, Java, and the Philippines. From May 1942 onward all operations were aimed at further expanding the area of influence up to the Midway, the Aleutians, and in the direction of Australia. In fact, it was in this new phase that the United States reaction began to be felt.

The decisive turning point in the conflict in the Pacific occurred late in the spring of 1942, with the air-sea battle of Midway (June 4-7), during which the Americans dealt a heavy blow to the supremacy of the Japanese, sinking four of their major aircraft carriers (the *Akagi*, the *Kaga*, the *Soryu*, and the *Hiryu*) as well as a cruiser. A month earlier (on May 7), another aircraft carrier (the *Shoho*) had been destroyed during the battle of the Coral Sea, the first in history to be fought by aircraft without the fleets coming within firing range of each other. These losses were particularly grave for Japan, considering the decisive role played by carrier-based aviation in a strategy founded on expansion in the context of a vast area of sea, and their weight was added to that of the psychological one represented by the first defeat. For the United States, on the other hand, not only did Midway represent a first victory, but it was also a revenge for Pearl Harbor. A revenge paid, however, at a high price, since the aircraft carrier *Yorktown* was also lost (the *Lexington* had been sunk during the battle of the Coral Sea), as well as the torpedo-boat destroyer *Hamman* and 150 of the 307 aircraft used in the battle.

Nevertheless, the battle of Midway, as well as representing the conclusion of the first phase of the hostilities in the Pacific, with the containing of the Japanese offensive, also had the effect of further confirming the modern combat plane's role of priority. In 1942, which was still a year of transition as far as the strengthening of the USAAF (U.S.Army Air Force) and the aviation of the U.S.Navy was concerned, aeronautical production was marked by a brusque increase compared to the 19,445 aircraft of every type built in the previous year. A total of 47,836 aircraft was built. This figure included 10,769 fighters and 12,627 bombers, of which 2,615 were four-engined and 7,247 were two-engined. Moreover, the production of engines increased from 58,181 in 1941, to 138,089 in 1942. At the same time, compared to the 100,000 men in service on December 8, 1941 (including both officers and ordinary troops), the figures for the following year reached more than a million.

It should also be remembered that when the United States entered the war, the USAAF's effective potential amounted to 3,305 aircraft ready for action, while those of the navy numbered approximately 3,000. Despite these numbers, it was not a particularly effective air force, considering that it was composed of obsolete models that were unable to compete with those of the German and Japanese adversaries.

Chronology

1941

May 6. The prototype of the Republic P-47 Thunderbolt, one of the most valid and powerful American fighters of the war, makes its maiden flight. In all, 15,683 were built in numerous versions, and the aircraft went into service early in 1943. After having fought on practically all fronts, it survived the conflict and served in the military aviations of approximately fifteen countries.

June. The strengthening of the American military aviation receives a strong impetus with the approval of a program that foresaw a force of 82 combat groups by June 1942, with allowances for 7,800 aircraft and 400,000 men.

August 1. The prototype of the Grumman XTBF-1 Avenger, a carrier-based torpedo plane, takes to the air. It was to become one of the protagonists of the air-sea battles in the Pacific. The Avenger went into service in the spring of 1942, and 9,836 were built in all. The aircraft remained in front-line service until 1954.

1942

May 21. The night fighter Northrop XP-61 makes its maiden flight. The P-61, christened Black Widow thanks to its deadly efficiency, went into action in the summer of 1944 on the Pacific front.

June 26. The Grumman XF6F-3, one of the U.S.Navy's best carrier-based fighters, makes its maiden flight. It went into service in January 1943 as the F6F Hellcat, and 12,272 were built in all. In the course of its intensive operative career, this aircraft shot down a total of 5,156 enemy aircraft.

September 21. The XB-29 prototype, ancestor of the greatest and most powerful strategic bomber of the entire conflict, takes to the air. In all, 3,970 B-29s were constructed. Two of them, in particular, hold a special place in aviation history: one christened *Enola Gay* which released the first atomic bomb in history on Hiroshima on August 6, 1945; and the other christened Bock's Car, which carried out a similar mission over Nagasaki three days later.

October 1. The first prototype of the P-59 Airacomet, the first American jet-propelled aircraft, takes to the air. It went into production in 1944, but never became operative.

CONSOLIDATED B-24D

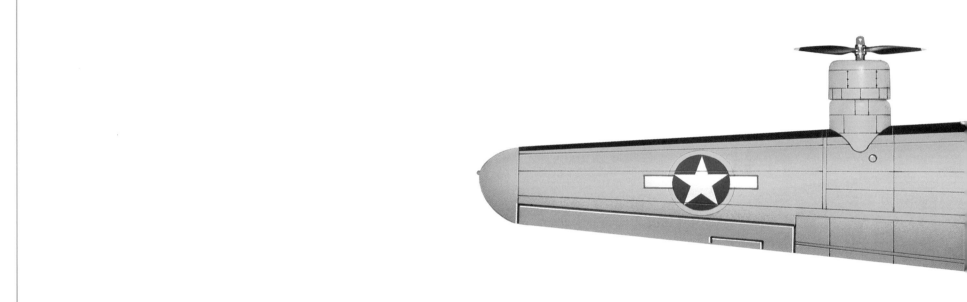

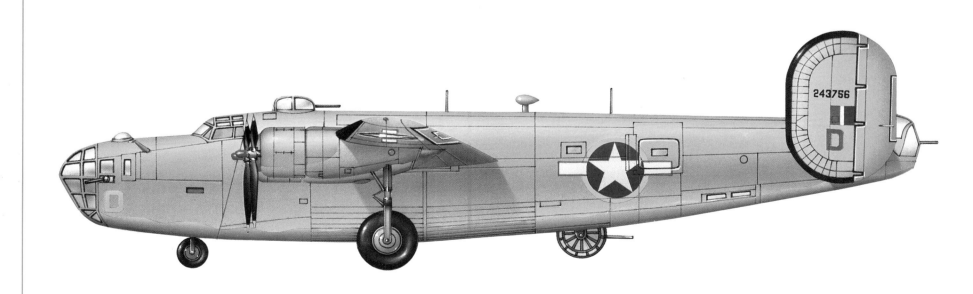

The second strategic bomber to be used in action by the United States, the B-24 Liberator never achieved the popularity of its companion and rival, the B-17. Nevertheless, the contribution that this large four-engine aircraft made to the course of the war was considerable, as was the quantity of aircraft produced greater than that of any other American combat plane in World War II. In all, a total of 18,188 came off the assembly lines prior to May 31, 1945. The quantitative ''importance'' of the Liberator can best be appreciated when compared with the production of the B-17 (12,731 built) and with that of the best British bomber, the Avro Lancaster (7,366). Used extensively on all fronts, the B-24 proved over all to be a versatile aircraft and, thanks to its excellent range, it was able to operate brilliantly in roles that were very different from its basic one, including transport, naval reconnaissance, and antisubmarine attack. The Liberator did not only serve bearing American insignia: the second major user was the British RAF, which received 1,694 in various versions, while other aircraft went to equip the Australian, Canadian, and South African air forces.

The project was launched by Consolidated in January 1939, on the basis of a request by the USAAC for a new heavy bomber with a performance that was generally superior to that of the Boeing B-17 in production at the time. Its main quality, however, was to be its range, and in order to satisfy this request to the full, the chief designer, Isaac M. Laddon, created a wing with advanced characteristics, which was greatly lengthened and provided with Davis laminar contours, around which the rest of the plane was literally constructed. The aircraft was a high wing monoplane with twin tail fins and rudders, tricycle forward landing gear, and was initially powered by four Pratt & Whitney R-1830-33 engines with two-stage mechanical superchargers, enclosed in a housing that was carefully studied from an aerodynamic point of view. The fuselage, which was very high, had sliding hatches that notably reduced the aircraft's drag.

On March 30 a contract was signed for the development of a full-scale model and a prototype, and nine months later, on December 29, 1939, the XB-24 made its maiden flight. In the meantime, seven YB-24 preseries aircraft had been ordered, as well as 36 B-24As of the initial production series. A further 175 aircraft had been ordered by France. However, the course of the war in Europe led to the French order being cancelled, and the aircraft were sent to Great Britain which, in the meantime, had also ordered 165 of the new bombers giving them the name that was also adopted in the United States: Liberator. The first of these took to the air on January 17, 1941, and deliveries began in March. Some of these aircraft were used for transport duty, but their use was subsequently extended to the RAF's Coastal Command.

In the meantime, the XB-24 prototype had been transformed into the XB-24B. The most substantial changes, excluding the strengthening of the defensive armament, consisted of more armor protection and, above all, in the adoption of engines provided with superchargers driven by exhaust gas. The latter change led to modifications in the structure of the engine nacelles, which assumed their characteristic oval shape. Nine aircraft of this type were completed with the designation B-24C, and from these was derived the most important production series version, the B-24D, for which a huge number of orders was issued during 1940 for a total of 2,738 aircraft. New assembly lines were opened in order to satisfy production requirements, and other manufacturers became involved in the program as well as Consolidated (these included Douglas, Ford, and North American). The B-24Ds (designated Liberator Mk.III by the RAF and PB4Y-1 by the U.S.Navy) were used as bombers by the USAAF from June 1942, and most of their initial service took place in the Middle East and the Pacific. The next version, the B-24E, was basically similar (with the exception of the propellers and other small details) and was the first to be built by Ford.

---

color plate

Consolidated B-24D 98th Bomb Group U.S.Army Air Force - North Africa 1943

Aircraft:	Consolidated B-24D
Nation:	USA
Manufacturer:	Consolidated Aircraft Corp.
Type:	Bomber
Year:	1942
Engine:	4 Pratt & Whitney R-1830-43 Twin Wasp, 14-cylinder radial, air-cooled, 1,200 hp
Wingspan:	110 ft (33.52 m)
Length:	66 ft 4 in (20.22 m)
Height:	17 ft 11 in (5.46 m)
Weight:	60,000 lb (27,216 kg) loaded
Maximum speed:	303 mph (488 km/h) at 25,000 ft (7,620 m)
Ceiling:	32,000 ft (9,750 m)
Range:	2,850 miles (4,585 km)
Armament:	10 machine guns; 8,830 lb (4,000 kg) of bombs
Crew:	8-10

A Consolidated B-24D in service on the Pacific front during a mission in New Guinea.

PETLYAKOV Pe-2

The Petlyakov Pe-2 was one of the most versatile combat planes to go into service with the Soviet air force in the course of World War II. Designed in 1938, this slim two-engine aircraft was not taken out of production until early in 1945, after the assembly lines had completed no fewer than 11,427. Its operative career was no less intense and continued for virtually the entire war in a great variety of roles: as well as being a standard tactical bomber (together with the equally effective Ilyushin Il-2), the Pe-2 also served brilliantly as a heavy fighter, reconnaissance plane, and night fighter. It succeeded in carrying out these roles successfully thanks to a continuous series of modernizations and strengthening of the basic airframe. Moreover, in the years immediately following the war, some of the final series were also sent to Czechoslovakia, Yugoslavia, and Poland.

The Pe-2 originated in 1938, when Vladimir Mikhailovic Petlyakov (a technician who had gained great experience working on projects by Andrei N. Tupolev) was charged with developing a high-altitude heavy fighter. The prototype (initially designated VI-100) was a low-wing two-engine monoplane, with double tail fins and retractable landing gear. It was powered by a pair of Klimov M.105 engines with superchargers, generating 1,050 hp each. A pressurized cockpit was planned, but the initial series of flight tests (the aircraft made its maiden flight between the end of 1939 and the beginning of 1940) went ahead without this being installed. Despite several faults, flight tests revealed the new aircraft to have excellent overall qualities, and in May 1940 it was decided to transform the prototype into a dive-bomber, with the new designation PB-100. The modifications (overall structural restrengthening, redimensioning of the wing, the abolition of the pressurized cockpit, and the adoption of aerodynamic brakes in the lower part of the half-wings) were carried out on the second prototype, which took to the air in June. On the twenty-third of the same month it was decided to put the new aircraft into mass production with the official designation of Petlyakov Pe-2.

The first aircraft of the initial series took to the air on November 18, 1940, and the bomber became operative in the spring of the following year. The dive-bomber version was merely the first of many other variants that were built in the course of production. Of these, mention should be made of the following: the Pe-2M (which took to the air in October 1941), fitted with more powerful engines and capable of carrying four 1,103 lb (500 kg) bombs internally; the Pe-3, a version adapted for use as an interceptor, night fighter, and reconnaissance plane, characterized by heavier offensive armament, which was increased from the four or five initial machine guns to include eventually two 20 mm cannons, three 12.7 mm and two 7.92 mm weapons; the Pe-2FT, the standard version from 1942 onward, lacking the bomb hold and diving brakes and armed with two cannons, two heavy machine guns, and two light ones. The final bomber versions were the Pe-2B and

A Petlyakov Pe-2 of the initial production series identifiable by the antenna situated well to the rear.

the Pe-2M, both dating to 1944: as well as numerous structural and aerodynamic improvements, the former was characterized by armament consisting of four machine guns and by UK-105PF engines generating 1,260 hp each, while the latter was characterized by armament consisting of three 20 mm cannons, a 4,415 lb (2,000 kg) bomb load, and UK-107A engines capable of generating 1,650 hp each.

Paradoxically, this successful aircraft was not very generous to its designer. Petlyakov, who had been released from prison where he had been held since 1937 in order to create the aircraft, lost his life on January 12, 1942, while on board the second production series aircraft of the Pe-2. This aircraft, used as a transport plane by his department, caught fire in flight and crashed to the ground, where it was completely destroyed.

---

color plate

Petlyakov Pe-2 Soviet Air Force - USSR 1943

Aircraft:	Petlyakov Pe-2
Nation:	USSR
Manufacturer:	State Industries
Type:	Bomber
Year:	1941
Engine:	2 Klimov M.105R, 12-cylinder V, liquid-cooled, 1,100 hp each
Wingspan:	56 ft 5 in (17.16 m)
Length:	42 ft 2 in (12.78 m)
Height:	11 ft 3 in (3.42 m)
Weight:	16,635 lb (7,536 kg)
Maximum speed:	335 mph (540 km/h) at 16,447 ft (5,000 m)
Ceiling:	28,947 ft (8,800 m)
Range:	816 miles (1,315 km)
Armament:	4-5 machine guns; 2,205 lb (1,000 kg) of bombs
Crew:	3

A formation of Petlyakov Pe.2 bombers taxiing on a snow-covered airport runway.

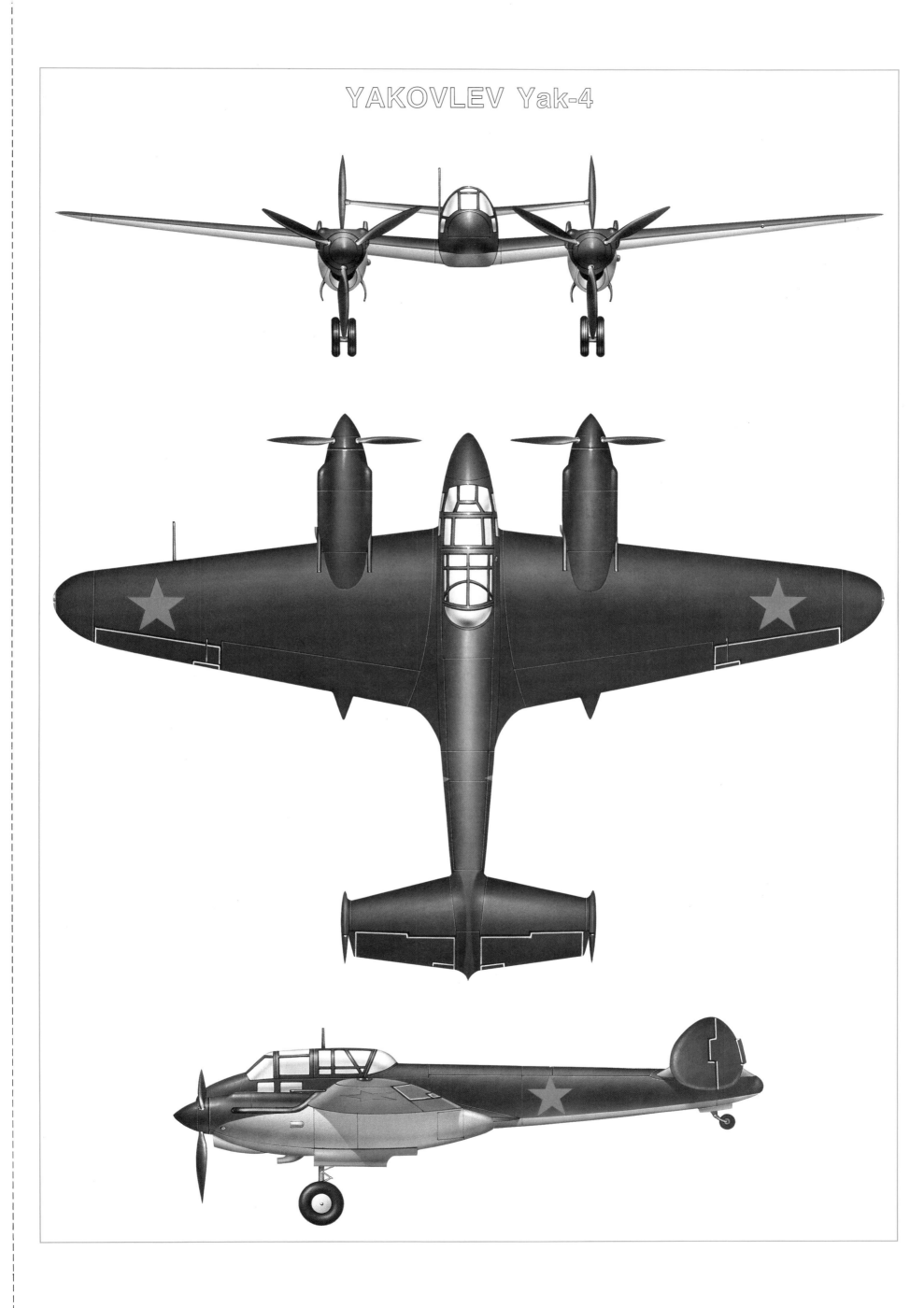

Aleksandr Sergheievic Yakovlev's first military project was initially designated Ya-22 (AIR-22) and appeared at the beginning of 1939. An elegant two-engine monoplane with retractable forward tricycle landing gear and double empennages, it was conceived as a long-range reconnaissance plane. The prototype made its maiden flight on February 22 of the same year, and its overall performance made such a good impression (especially as far as speed was concerned) that it was decided to alter the project in order to construct a light bomber, suitable also for carrying out the role of ground attack.

The two-engine aircraft was redesignated BB-22, although the changes necessary for the new role that had been requested led to a large series of modifications, which occupied the designer for many months. The housing of the two-man crew had to be changed, as well as the position of the armament and the fuel tanks, and an internal bomb hold had to be created. The first BB-22 was completed on the final day of the year and made its maiden flight on January 20, 1940. At the same time, it was decided to construct another two prototypes, one for photographic reconnaissance (R-12), and the other for long-range fighter escort (I-29). During flight tests and operative evaluations, the BB-22 (powered by a pair of Klimov M.103 engines generating 960 hp each) gave excellent proof of its performance, especially as far as its speed was concerned, reaching a maximum speed of 329 mph (530 km/h) at sea level. Moreover, it had a range of 496 miles (800 km) and a service ceiling of 28,947 ft (8,800 m).

During the course of the year the project (officially designated Yak-2) was improved still further. The new version was designated Yak-4 and went into production in the autumn. Compared to the previous version, the housing for the crew and the armor were improved, while the adoption of the more powerful Klimov M.105 engines led to a further improvement in the aircraft's performance and allowed for an increase in the bomb load. In all, approximately

600 two-engine Yakovlevs came off the production lines, most them Yak-4s. However, their operative service did not prove to be particularly satisfactory. The aircraft were very vulnerable, especially when compared with the Ilyushin Il-2s, which were stronger and more protected.

Because of combat experiences the two-engine Yak's career was cut short: production ceased in 1942, and the surviving aircraft were removed from front-line service and relegated to high-altitude reconnaissance missions. They remained operative in this role until the end of the war.

color plate
Yakovlev Yak-4 Soviet Air Force - USSR 1942

Aircraft:	Yakovlev Yak-4
Nation:	USSR
Manufacturer:	State Industries
Type:	Attack
Year:	1941
Engine:	2 Klimov M.105R, 12-cylinder V, liquid-cooled, 1,050 hp each
Wingspan:	46 ft (14.00 m)
Length:	30 ft 8 in (9.34 m)
Height:	—
Weight:	11,479 lb (5,200 kg)
Maximum speed:	335 mph (540 km/h) at 16,447 ft (5,000 m)
Ceiling:	31,250 ft (9,500 m)
Range:	745 miles (1,200 km)
Armament:	3 machine guns; 1,329 lb (600 kg) of bombs
Crew:	2

A Yak-4 which was damaged and captured by the German troops during the invasion of Russia.

THE SOVIET UNION

When the German attack of June 1941 took place, the Soviet military aviation was in an extremely inferior position, especially as far as quality was concerned. At that time, the units of the VVS (Voenno Vosnusniye Sili) were still undergoing reorganization, and they were paradoxically provided with the same aircraft as ten years before, considering that the new models that were to replace them were not yet operative, either because they were in an experimental phase or production had not yet been launched. The Luftwaffe gained supremacy in the air right from the start and was to retain it in a decisive way. The factor that upset this balance was the arrival of winter, which greatly slowed down the air operations of both sides, favoring the Red Army in the long term by giving it time for strengthening and reorganization.

In fact, it was at this time that the Russians put into practice one of the most important strategical decisions of the war: the transfer of the war industry away from the area of the front, the only possible move allowing the reorganization of the industrial network and to make it competitive once more. During the winter months more than 600 factories were moved to areas that were considered safe: the Volga region, the Urals, and western Siberia. Entire aircraft and engine factories were dismantled and rebuilt, often in emergency conditions, and research and study centers were transferred with them.

This was a long and complex process, and together with many difficulties, it caused a great drop in aeronautical production, which further slowed the reequipping of the units with more advanced and competitive aircraft. In fact, although the total number of aircraft of all types produced in 1941 reached 15,735, production literally collapsed in the second half of the year, and this situation continued throughout the early months of 1942: 1,039 aircraft were produced in January, 915 in February, and 1,647 in March. However, in the end, the results compensated for the immense effort. The beginning of the complete recovery occurred in 1942, with productivity going ahead to the full. The recovery was not only quantitative (in the whole year no fewer than 25,400 aircraft of all types came off the assembly lines, in addition to 38,000 aircraft engines), but also, and above all, qualitative, with the appearance of planes that were the result of new projects. These contributed to reestablishing the balance as far as the German Luftwaffe was concerned, especially in the fighter and attack sectors.

The process of altering the aeronautical industry went ahead at the same time, with the increasing introduction of mechanization and the rationalization both of the assembly lines and production, marked by the gradual passage from traditional methods of construction in wood to more modern ones using metal not only for the airframes, but also for the covering.

The huge contribution made by the other Allies in terms of means and materials also formed part of this process. In the aeronautical field in particular, from 1941 to 1945, the United States alone sent approximately 15,000 aircraft of all types to the Soviet Union, and no fewer than 500 million worth of machinery, equipment, and raw materials, such as steel, copper, and aluminum. This resulted in the Soviet industrial network making a further leap forward, and it was not only able to construct the huge total of 125,000 aircraft in the course of the entire conflict, reaching a production rate of 41,800 per year in 1945, but also to achieve complete autonomy and total competitiveness. These were fundamental premises for the remarkable developments that were to take place immediately after the war.

Chronology

1941

January 28. The Tupolev ANT-58 makes its maiden flight. The Tu-2 was to be developed from its prototype. In number and importance, this aircraft was the second medium bomber built in the Soviet Union during the conflict. It remained in production from 1942 to 1948, and in service until the end of the 1950s.

June 22. Hitler launches Operation Barbarossa, the massive attack on the Soviet Union that extended from the Baltic to the Black Sea.

June 23. In order to combat the German invasion, the Soviet national airline (Aeroflot) is mobilized: aircraft and personnel are placed at the disposal of the armed forces to carry out transport duties. Action around Leningrad was particularly intense between October and December.

August 7/8. Soviet naval aviation Il-4 bombers carry out a raid on Berlin. The mission was a reprisal for the massive bombing raids carried out by the Luftwaffe on Moscow, the first of which took place on the night of July 21/22.

August 27. First contact between Soviet aircraft and the aircraft of the Italian Expeditionary Corps in the Soviet Union (CSIR). The command of this force had been organized on July 30 to support the German invasion.

1942

March. The prototype of the Lavochkin La-5, one of the best Soviet fighters of the conflict, takes to the air. The aircraft was derived from the previous LaGG-3 model (conceived in 1938), from which it differed mainly in the adoption of a large and powerful radial engine. Approximately 15,000 of the La-5 series aircraft were built, the last of which fought in Korea in 1950.

July. The Il-2M3 variant of the famous Ilyushin Il-2 attack plane goes into action. It was fitted with a more powerful engine, was better armed, and had a second crew member. This was the version of which the most aircraft were built, including more than 35,000 Sturmoviks that came off the assembly lines.

August. The first Yakovlev Yak-9 fighters go into service. This was the final variant of the series of combat planes built by Aleksandr Sergheievic Yakovlev, that originated with the Yak-1 model. This family of aircraft was the one that was most widely used by the Soviet Union in the course of the conflict.

MITSUBISHI G4M3

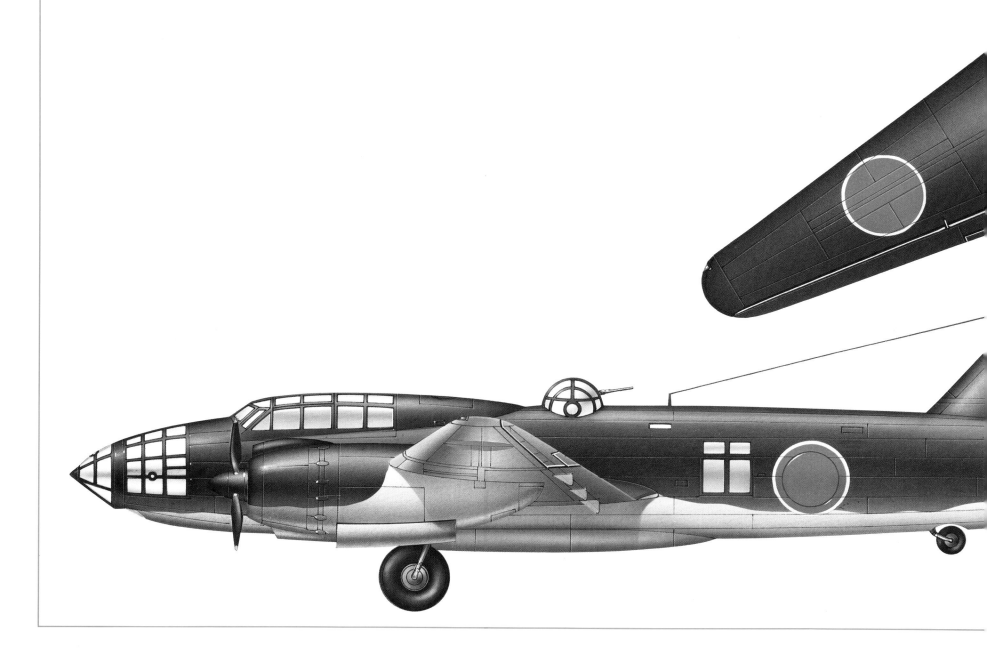

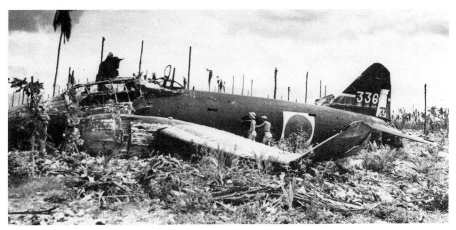

A wrecked Betty at Munda airport in the Solomon Islands.

Undoubtedly the most famous Japanese bomber of the war, the Mitsubishi G4M was one of the protagonists of the conflict in the Pacific. Between October 1939 and August 1945, no fewer than 2,445 of these large two-engine aircraft came off the assembly lines, the largest quantity for a plane in this category, and their operative career lasted from the first day of the conflict to the last. In fact, on August 19, 1945, two G4M1s painted white and bearing green crosses surrender in place of the Rising Sun insignia carried the Japanese surrender committee to Ie-Shima.

In 1937 the Imperial Navy issued the specifications that gave rise to the G4M. They called for the construction of a land-based bomber with characteristics superior to those of the G3M, which was then about to go into service. These included a maximum speed of 248 mph (400 km/h) at an altitude of 9,868 ft (3,000 m) and a range of no less than 2,980 miles (4,800 km) without bombload and 2,297 miles (3,700 km) with a torpedo weighing 1,766 lb (800 kg). Mitsubishi started work on the project immediately, and the first of two prototypes took to the air on October 23, 1939. The initial series of tests proved that the designer, Kiro Honjo, had succeeded in satisfying the rigid specifications brilliantly: the aircraft lacked any intrinsic faults, and above all it had no difficulty in surpassing the speed and range that had been requested. In fact, the second prototype reached a maximum speed of 276 mph (445 km/h) and a range of over 3,415 miles (5,500 km). The aircraft was a large all-metal middle-wing monoplane with retractable rear tricycle landing gear. It was powered initially by a pair of 1,530 hp Mitsubishi Kasei 11 radial engines.

However, mass production did not commence immediately. Operative experiences during the war in China had revealed the lack of a long-range combat plane capable of escorting the bombers during their missions in enemy territory. Considering the G4M's excellent qualities, a proposal was made to develop a heavy fighter escort aircraft from it. Redesignated G6M1 and armed with four 20 mm cannons (two of which were situated in the

hold) plus a 7.7 mm machine gun, 30 of these aircraft were built in 1940. However, once they went into service their performance proved to be disappointing, due to the great disadvantages caused by an increase in weight and by the consequent reduction in fuel capacity. These aircraft were thus modified for use as trainers, and subsequently for transport.

In the same year, authorization for the production of the aircraft as a bomber was finally granted, and the first of the initial variant came off the assembly lines in April 1941. The aircraft made its operative debut in China a few weeks later, providing combat experience for the crews that was to prove extremely useful at the beginning of the subsequent conflict.

During the early months of the war in the Pacific, and throughout the first year, the Mitsubishi bombers scored some great successes, due above all to their remarkable range. These included a role in the mission that led to the sinking of the British battleships *Prince of Wales* and *Repulse* on December 10, 1941. However, their operative career also revealed what was to prove to be the G4M's greatest fault: the absence of protective armor and the lack of self-sealing fuel tanks. The latter, together with the fact that the aircraft caught fire easily, earned the "Betty" (as the bomber was known in the Allies' code) the unfortunate nickname of "Flying Cigar." These defects were also present in the second version, the G4M2, of which 1,154 were built beginning in November 1942. The main differences between the two versions lay in their armament and engines. In fact, the problems were solved only in the final variant, the G4M3, although only 60 were built in all, starting in late 1943.

---

color plate

Mitsubishi G4M3 Yokosuka Chutai - Imperial Japanese Army Air Force - Japan 1945

Aircraft:	Mitsubishi G4M1
Nation:	Japan
Manufacturer:	Mitsubishi Jukogyo KK
Type:	Bomber
Year:	1941
Engine:	2 Mitsubishi Mk4A Kasei 11, 14-cylinder radial, 1,530 hp each
Wingspan:	82 ft (25 m)
Length:	65 ft 7 1/2 in (20 m)
Height:	19 ft 8 in (6 m)
Weight:	20,944 lb (9,500 kg) loaded
Maximum speed:	266 mph (428 km/h) at 13,780 ft (4,200 m)
Ceiling:	29,000 ft (8,840 m)
Range:	3,748 miles (6,030 km)
Armament:	1 × 20 mm cannon; 4 machine guns; 1,766 lb (800 kg) of bombs
Crew:	7

A Mitsubishi G4M2 Betty during evaluations by Allied technicians after the end of the war.

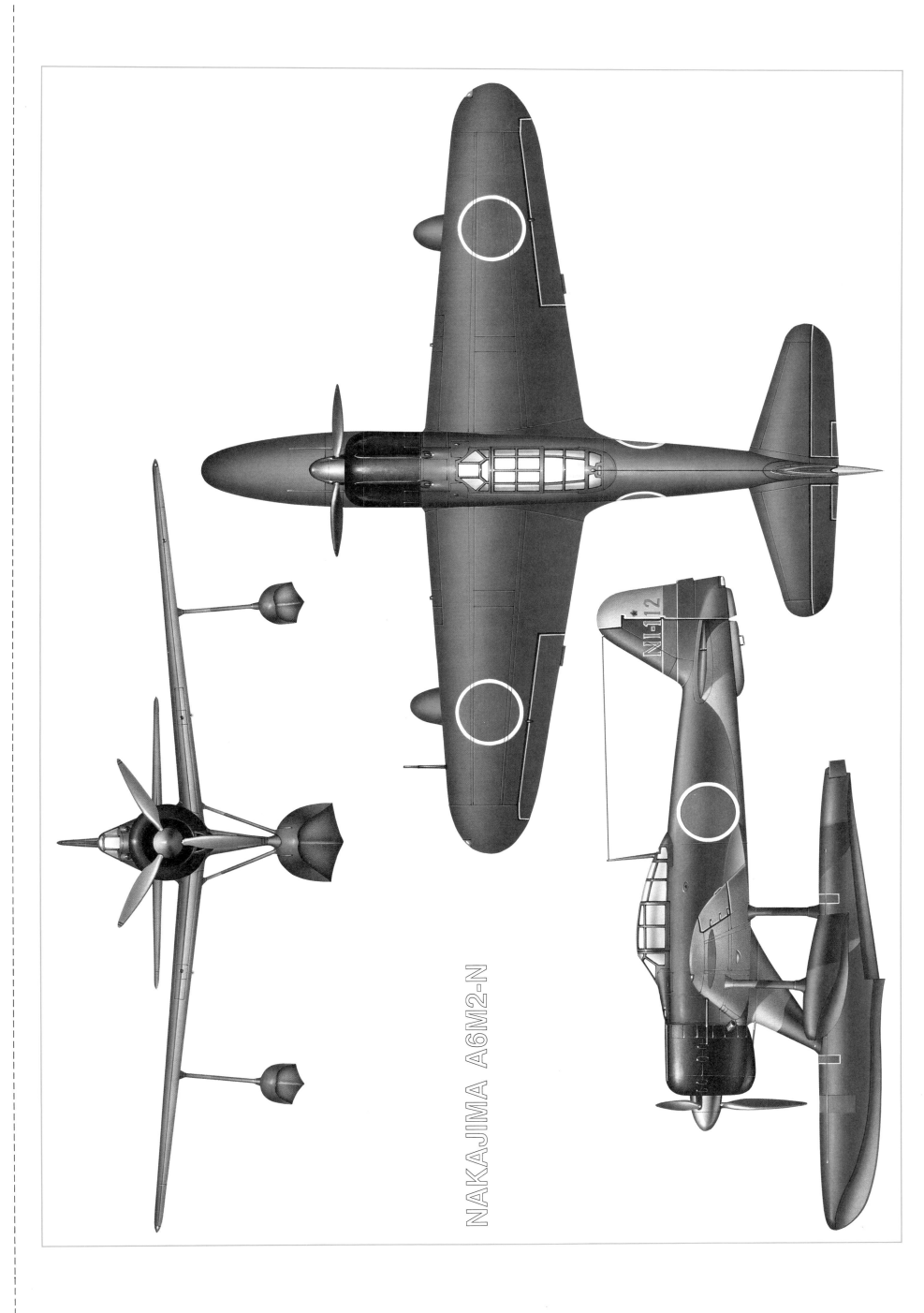

NAKAJIMA A6M2-N

In 1940, the need for a single-seater fighter seaplane was strongly felt by the Japanese Imperial Navy. In fact, an aircraft of this type was to prove fundamental not only in supporting the amphibious operations that the general staff was already planning but also for use at military bases on small islands where the building of runways was impossible. The first manufacturer to respond to the navy's request was Kawanishi, which began to study the project that was to give rise to the powerful N1K Kyofu. However, the advanced nature of the technical solutions adopted in this aircraft (especially the use of a pair of contrarotating propellers) and the problems in preparing the aircraft that soon became evident led to great delays in the program, and therefore the technical authorities of the Imperial Navy asked Nakajima to develop a seaplane version of the most famous fighter in service at the time: the Mitsubishi A6M Reisen, the famous Zero. In fact, the A6M2-N (known as ''Rufe'' in the Allies' code) derived from this aircraft, and although it did not prove to be exceptional it served a useful role, especially during the initial phases of the war in the Pacific.

The construction of the aircraft did not pose any particular problems, considering the remarkable qualities of the airframe from which it was derived. Nakajima's technicians, who had already helped Mitsubishi with the construction of the Zero, used an A6M2 Model II as their base and work began in February 1941. In practice, the prototype maintained almost the entire structure and configuration of the original fighter, apart from the obvious differences due to the fitting of a large central float and of two smaller side floats: the landing gear was removed and the wheel housing covered, while a small ventral fin was added to the tail to increase stability. To compensate for the lack of supplementary external fuel tanks (which could no longer be installed in the belly of the fuselage) an auxiliary fuel tank was installed inside the largest float. The aircraft's engine was identical to that of the original model, as was its armament.

The prototype of the A6M2-N made its maiden flight on December 7, 1941, the very same day that Japan entered the war, and a series of flight tests and evaluations did not reveal any particular problems: despite an increase in overall weight and the high aerodynamic drag of the floats, the fighter proved to be very fast and, above all, extremely maneuverable. From December 1941 to September 1943, a total of 327 A6M2s came off the assembly lines.

The aircraft began its operative career the following year in the Solomon Islands, and it proved to be reasonably successful. However, the appearance of the more powerful and modern Allied fighters revealed the aircraft's inferiority and its inability to sustain front-line roles. During the final months of the war, many A6M2-Ns were used as trainers for the more powerful Kawanishi N1K1.

color plate

Nakajima A6M2-N 802 Kokutai Japanese Imperial Navy Air Force - Solomon Islands 1943

Aircraft:	Nakajima A6M2-N
Nation:	Japan
Manufacturer:	Nakajima Hikoki KK
Type:	Fighter
Year:	1942
Engine:	Nakajima NK1C Sakae 12, 14-cylinder radial, air-cooled, 950 hp
Wingspan:	39 ft 4 1/2 in (12 m)
Length:	33 ft 2 in (10.10 m)
Height:	14 ft 1 in (4.30 m)
Weight:	6,349 lb (2,895 kg)
Maximum speed:	270 mph (434 km/h) at 16,447 ft (5,000 m)
Ceiling:	32,810 ft (10,000 m)
Range:	1,107 miles (1,780 km)
Armament:	2 × 20 mm cannon; 2 machine guns; 264 lb (120 kg) of bombs
Crew:	1

A Nakajima A6M2-N of the Sasebo Kokutai in flight over Sasebo Harbor.

KAWASAKI Ki-48-IIb

The appearance of the Tupolev SB-2 in China led to the construction of the Kawasaki Ki-48 in Japan. In fact, the general staff of the Imperial Army was so impressed by the speed of the two-engine Soviet aircraft (which was equal to that of the Nakajima Ki-27, the latest fighter to go into service) that an immediate request was made to the aeronautical industry for the creation of a light bomber with a similar performance. From July 1940 to October 1944, no fewer than 1,977 Ki-48s came off the assembly lines, a remarkable number considering that in practice, with the changing situations presented by the world war, the aircraft actually proved to be extremely vulnerable and an easy prey for the enemy.

In December 1937 the Imperial Army issued the specifications. These were especially severe, calling for a maximum speed of 298 mph (480 km/h) at an altitude of 9,868 ft (3,000 m); a cruising speed of 217 mph (350 km/h) at the same altitude; ascent to 16,447 ft (5,000 m) in 10 minutes; a bomb load of 883 lb (400 kg); defensive armament consisting of three to four machine guns. Moreover, it was to be capable of operating in difficult weather conditions and at freezing temperatures. The project was entrusted to Takeo Doi, the technician who was also working on the construction of the Ki-45 heavy bomber, and preliminary studies began in January 1938. However, this phase was hampered by difficulties that emerged in the bomber program, and the first of the four Ki-48 prototypes did not take to the air until July of the following year. It was a middle cantilever wing monoplane with retractable rear tricycle landing gear. It was powered initially by a pair of 950 hp Nakajima Ha-25 radial engines. However, a series of problems emerged during the initial flight tests, the most worrying of which concerned strong tail vibrations. Several structural alterations were necessary to solve the problem. Production of the Ki-48-I, the initial variant, was launched toward the end of 1939, although it was not until the summer of 1940 that the first aircraft came off the assembly lines (following the construction of five preseries planes). They were subsequently sent to China in the autumn. Kawasaki built a total of 557 aircraft, which were subdivided into two series, the Ia and the Ib, which differed only in small details.

At the beginning of 1942 (after the aircraft's relative inadequacy compared to the Allied fighters had become apparent), it was decided to build a second version (the Ki-48-II) with more powerful engines, provided with more effective defense and with the maximum bomb load increased to 1,766 lb (800 kg). In February 1942 three prototypes were completed and production commenced in April. This reached a total of 1,408 aircraft, divided into three subvariants: the IIa; the IIb (transformed into a dive-bomber); the IIc, similar to the first but with its defensive armament strengthened by the addition of an extra 7.7 mm machine gun in a forward position and the adoption of a 12.7 mm weapon on the aircraft's back. This series, which was the last, appeared in 1943, although even these improvements did not render the aircraft competitive. Production came to a definitive close in October of the following year, and the Ki-48 ended its career by being employed in the suicide attacks that occurred in the final months of the conflict. The Ki-48 was known as "Lily" in the Allies' code.

---

color plate

Kawasaki Ki-48-IIb 8th Sentai 2nd Chutai Japanese Imperial Army Air Force - Burma 1943

The Kawasaki Ki-48 twin-engine bomber was produced in many variants which differed only in small details.

A close-up of the canopy of a Ki-48.

Aircraft:	Kawasaki Ki-48-IIa
Nation:	Japan
Manufacturer:	Kawasaki Kokuki Kogyo KK
Type:	Bomber
Year:	1942
Engine:	2 Nakajima Ha-115, 14-cylinder radial, air-cooled, 1,150 hp each
Wingspan:	57 ft 3 in (17.45 m)
Length:	41 ft 10 in (12.75 m)
Height:	12 ft 6 in (3.80 m)
Weight:	14,880 lb (6,763 kg) loaded
Maximum speed:	314 mph (505 km/h) at 18,375 ft (5,600 m)
Ceiling:	33,135 ft (10,100 m)
Range:	1,491 miles (2,400 km)
Armament:	3 machine guns; 1,766 lb (800 kg) of bombs
Crew:	4

JAPAN

The first phase of the war in the Pacific lasted more or less six months, from Pearl Harbor to Midway. Until late in the spring of 1942, the Empire of the Rising Sun managed to achieve all the objectives established for the constitution of the "sphere of common prosperity of Great Eastern Asia," spreading across Malaysia, Burma, Java, and the Philippines. The advance was virtually impossible to halt and was marked by clamorous successes. The Allies, still weak and disorganized, were able to do very little.

From May 1942 onward, operations were directed toward further expansion in the area of influence up to the Midway islands, the Aleutians, and in the direction of Australia. However, it was in fact at Midway, those two small islands that represented the advance guard of American territory, that Japanese power received its first great setback. The air-sea battle, which came to a climax between June 4 and June 7, 1942, and in which the Japanese participated with a force of more than 180 ships and 589 aircraft, brusquely redressed the balance, not only due to the material effects of the encounter, but also to the psychological ones as far as both the adversaries were concerned.

The Americans emerged from Midway galvanized in their desire for revenge and backed by an industrial network that had no difficulties in replacing losses; the situation in Japan was the complete opposite. The Imperial fleet lost four of its precious aircraft carriers, along with their air groups and, above all, a large part of the most highly trained and effective crews available, perhaps the most difficult component to replace. Moreover the defeat·greatly damaged the prestige of the Japanese air force in Japan, which had been believed invincible up till then, with strong repercussions in public opinion that proved impossible to control. On a strategic level, the direct consequence of Midway was the renouncement by the Japanese of plans for the conquest of the Fiji Islands, Port Moresby, Samoa, New Caledonia, and Australia. In short, the Empire of Rising Sun found itself forced to abandon the offensive and to defend itself much earlier than its strategists had foreseen.

All this did not mean a slowing down in the war effort. Anything but. In the aeronautical field quantitative and qualitative progress was made at an extremely high level as far as the production of machines and engines was concerned, although it was practically impossible for the Imperial Navy's aviation, as well as that of the Army, to replace the slow hemorrhage of able and trained veterans with pilots and crew who were similarly prepared. The aeronautical production figures for the first two years of the war are the clearest indication of how great Japan's industrial potential was: in 1941, a total of 5,080 aircraft of all types came off the assembly lines (including 1,080 fighters and 1,461 bombers); moreover, in the same year, the production of propellers and aircraft engines totaled 12,621 and 12,151 respectively; in 1942, aeronautical production almost doubled, with a total of 8,861 aircraft, of which 2,935 were fighters and 2,433 were bombers, while 16,999 engines and 22,362 propellers were built. It should be mentioned that, in 1938, the Japanese aeronautical industry had built 3,201 aircraft of all types, a figure that increased to 4,467 in 1939, and to 4,768 in 1940.

Chronology

1941

January. The long range seaplane Kawanishi H8K1 makes its maiden flight. It was the final version of a project that originated in 1933. This large four-engine aircraft was one of the most effective in its category to be put into service by the Japanese, and a total of 215 was built between 1938 and 1942. The Kawanishi H8K1 proved to be particularly effective in naval reconnaissance missions.

December. The prototype of the Kawasaki Ki-61 Hien, the only Japanese fighter provided with an in-line liquid-cooled engine (the Daimler Benz DB 601A, built on license), begins test; 3,078 aircraft were built. Their operative service began in February 1943 and continued for the entire duration of the war. However, although it was generally effective, this fighter never proved to be particularly competitive.

1942

February. Three prototypes of the second version of the two-engine Kawasaki Ki-48 bomber are completed. The Ki-48-II had more powerful engines, was provided with more effective defensive protection, and its maximum bomb load was increased to 1,766 lb (800 kg). The production of the series began in April, reaching a total of 1,408 aircraft in three subvariants: the IIa, the IIb (transformed into a dive-bomber); the IIc, which was similar to the first but its defensive armament was increased by another 7.7 mm machine gun in a forward position and the installation of a 12.7 mm caliber weapon on the back.

September. Production of the Nakajima Ki-49-II Donryu is launched. Fitted with more powerful engines and better armed, it was the second variant of the heavy bomber developed to replace the Mitsubishi Ki-21 in the Imperial Army aviation; 667 aircraft were completed in two main subseries, and production ceased in December 1944, bringing the overall total to 819.

Autumn. A new variant of the famous Aichi D3A dive-bomber goes into service. This was the D3A2, provided with a 1,300 hp Kinsei engine, larger fuel tanks, and other improvements. Approximately 1,000 were built; they were initially assigned to the smaller aircraft carriers and were then used by ground-based units.

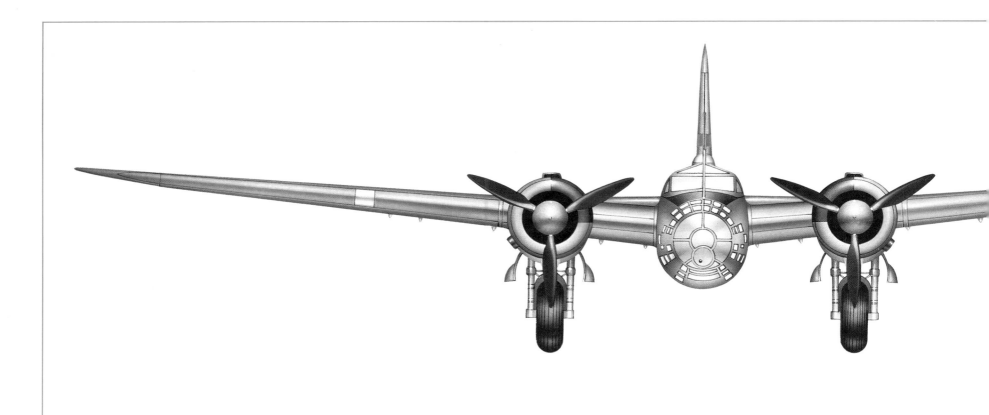

NAKAJIMA Ki-49

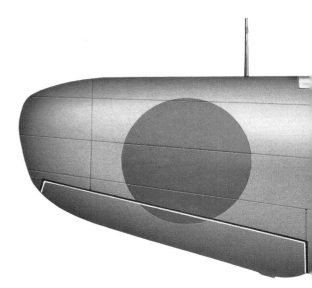

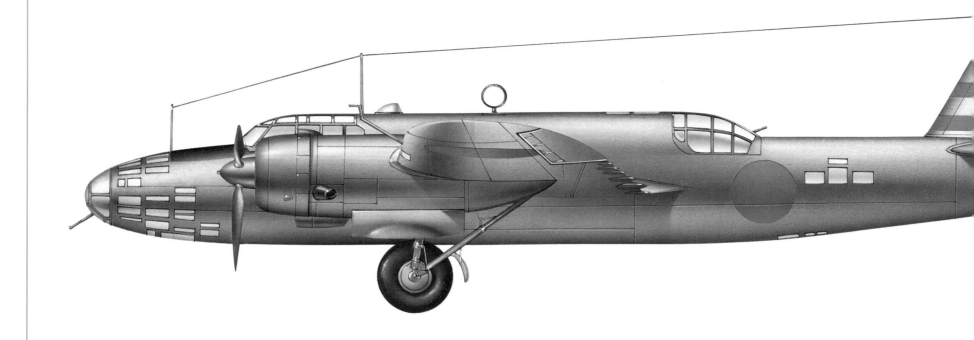

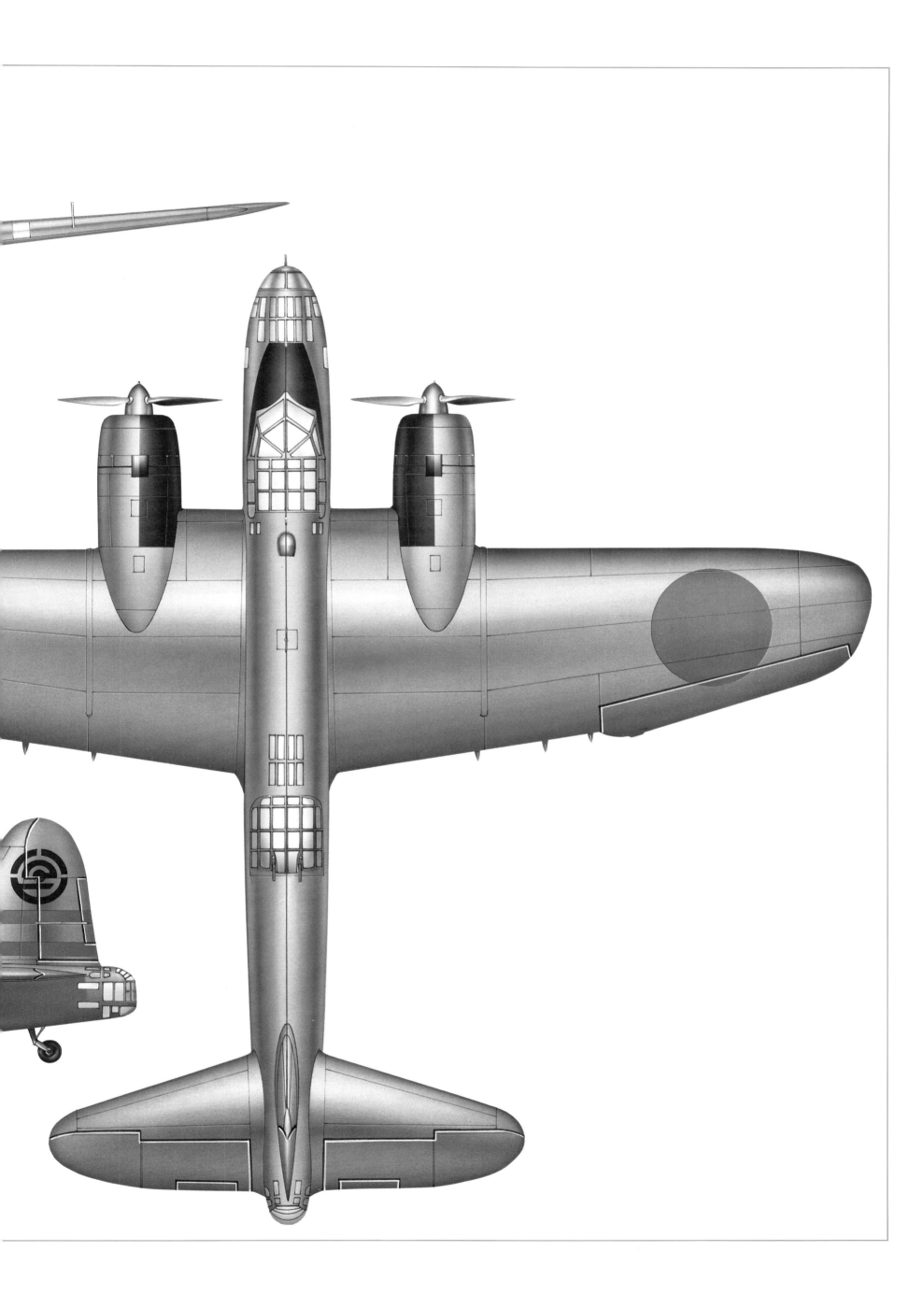

Christened Donryu (Dragon of the Storms), the Nakajima Ki-49 was developed in 1938 to replace the Mitsubishi Ki-21, which was just going into service at the time. However, this aim was not fulfilled, in that the new bomber proved to be generally inferior: it lacked power, and its performance was not exceptional. Above all, it was provided with insufficient defensive armament, which made it easy prey for enemy fighters. Nevertheless, production went ahead for four years, from December 1940 until December 1944, with a total of 819 aircraft being built in two major variants.

The specifications that gave rise to the Ki-49 were issued at the beginning of 1938. The Imperial Army wanted a two-engine heavy bomber capable of carrying out its missions without a fighter escort. The aircraft was therefore to be especially fast and well armed. Moreover, a maximum speed of 310 mph (500 km/h) and a range of 1,863 miles (3,000 km) were requested, while the offensive armament was to amount to 2,205 lb (1,000 kg) of bombs and the defensive armament foresaw the installation of a 20 mm cannon in a turret on the aircraft's back.

The project was launched by Nakajima's technicians toward the summer, and the first of the three prototypes was ready within a year and made its maiden flight in August 1939. It was a large monoplane with middle cantilever wing and retractable rear tricycle landing gear, powered initially by two 950 hp Nakajima Ha-5 KAI radial engines. The other two prototypes and seven preseries aircraft, built between January and December 1940, were fitted with two 1,450 hp Nakajima Ha-41 engines, which remarkably improved their performance.

However, evaluations and operative tests lasted much longer than expected. The war in China had revealed the need for a fighter escort plane with a sufficient range to accompany bombers throughout their long missions, and as in the case of the Mitsubishi G4M, the general staff of the Imperial Army requested that a version of the heavy fighter be built. This was designated Ki-58, and between December 1940 and March 1941 Nakajima built three prototypes. These aircraft were characterized by the elimination of the bomb hold, an increase in armour, and heavier armament, which included five 20 mm cannons and three 12.7 mm machine guns. However, the program was abandoned, and not until March 1941 was production of the Ki-49 as a bomber launched. The first aircraft of the initial Ki-49-I series came off the assembly lines in August, and their operative career began in the autumn on the Chinese front.

However, the imminence of the new conflict led to the construction of a new variant with more powerful engines and better armament. This was the Ki-49-II, which did not appear until 1942, when the war was already at an advanced stage. Production began in September (following the construction of the last of the 129 Ki-49-Is in August, and after two new prototypes had been

built), and a total of 667 aircraft was built in all (50 of which were constructed by Tachikawa) in two subseries, the IIa and the IIb, which differed only in their defensive armament. These aircraft were employed extensively, although in the course of their career their original faults were never eliminated, and these faults became even more apparent when the aircraft were faced with the more advanced Allied fighters. In 1943 an attempt at improvement was made with a third version, the Ki-49-III, fitted with new 2,420 hp Nakajima Ha-117 engines. However, between March and December of the same year only six prototypes were built, and they never went beyond the experimental phase due to problems caused by the new engines. Of the experimental versions, the Ki-80 (two prototypes were completed in October 1941) should be mentioned. In theory it was to carry out the role of guide in indicating targets for bombers.

A preproduction Nakajima aircraft in flight.

color plate
Nakajima Ki-49 Hamamatsu Army Flying School, Japanese Imperial Army Air Force - Japan 1944

Aircraft:	Nakajima Ki-49-IIb
Nation:	Japan
Manufacturer:	Nakajima Hikoki KK
Type:	Bomber
Year:	1942
Engine:	2 Nakajima Ha-109, 14-cylinder radial. air-cooled, 1,450 hp each
Wingspan:	67 ft (20.42 m)
Length:	54 ft 1 1/2 in (16.50 m)
Height:	13 ft 11 in (4.25 m)
Weight:	25,133 lb (11,424 kg) loaded
Maximum speed:	306 mph (492 km/h) at 16,447 ft (5,000 m)
Ceiling:	30,510 ft (9,300 m)
Range:	1,833 miles (2,950 km)
Armament:	1 × 20 mm cannon; 5 machine guns; 2,205 lb (1,000 kg) of bombs
Crew:	8

A Nakajima Ki-49 of the Hamamatsu Flying School.

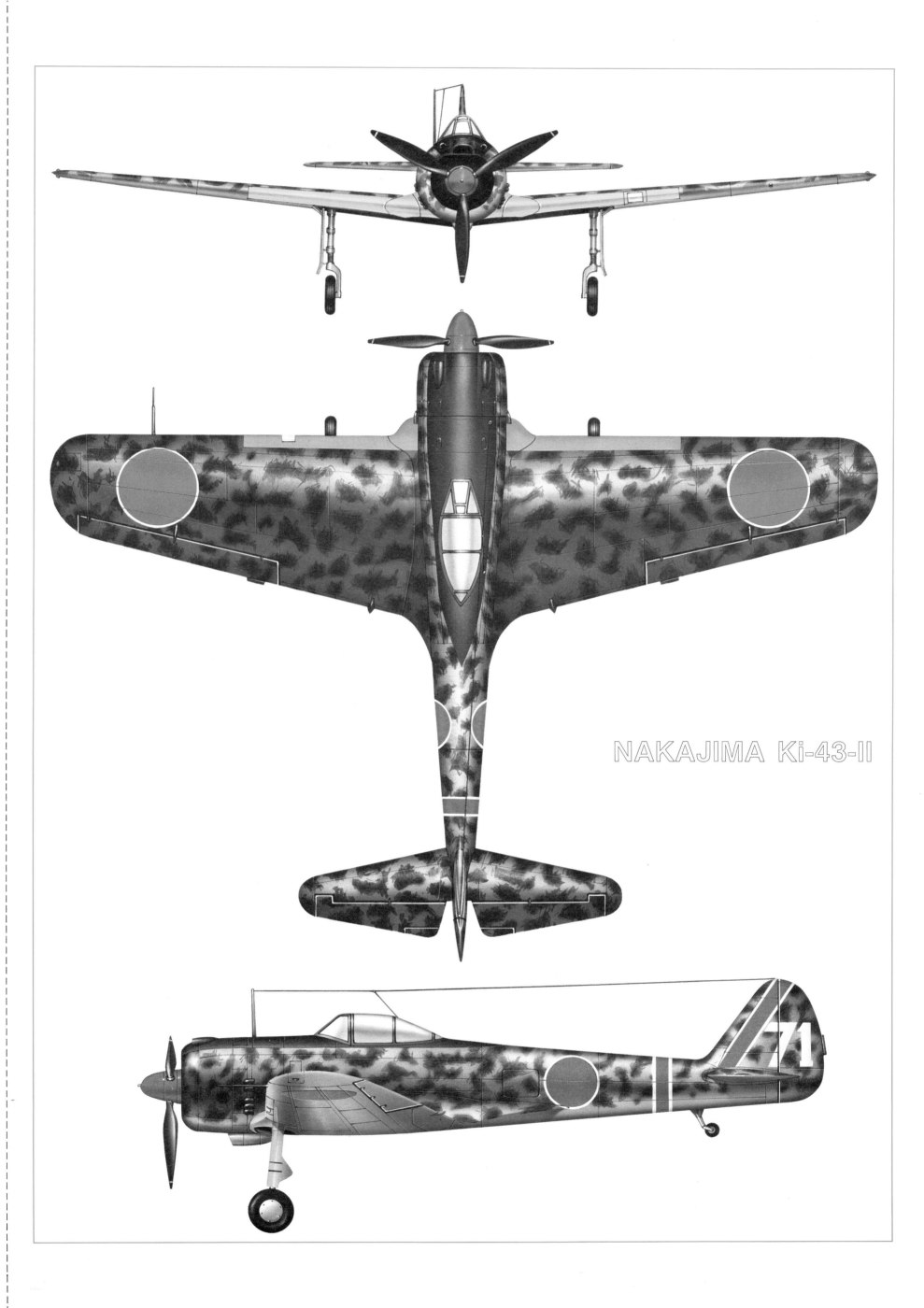

NAKAJIMA Ki-43-II

The Nakajima Ki-43 succeeded the Ki-27 as the Imperial Army's standard fighter and was created at more or less the same time as the Mitsubishi A6M Zero. Like its counterpart in the navy, it was the first advanced Japanese combat plane to be employed in the Pacific. Christened Hayabusa (Peregrine Falcon), the Ki-43 had a long and intensive operative career that lasted practically till the end of the war. Its moment of glory occurred during the first year of the conflict when, faced with less effective adversaries, the Nakajima Ki-43 fighter earned the reputation of being invincible.

The project was launched in December 1937 on the basis of specifications issued by the army requesting the construction of a modern fighter to replace the Ki-27. This fighter was to have a maximum speed of 310 mph (500 km/h); to be capable of reaching 16,447 ft (5,000 m) in five minutes; to have a range of 496 miles (800 km); and armament consisting of two 7.7 mm machine guns. Moreover, the new aircraft was to be provided with great maneuverability, equal to if not greater than that of the model it was to replace.

The project was entrusted to a team headed by Hideo Itokawa, and studies for the construction of a prototype lasted for exactly one year. In January 1939 the first of three experimental aircraft made its maiden flight, followed by the other two within the next couple of months. The aircraft was a low cantilever wing monoplane with retractable rear tricycle landing gear and was powered initially by a 975 hp Nakajima Ha-25 radial engine. Although no great problems emerged from the series of tests, the fighter's maneuverability was severely criticized by Imperial Army technicians during operational evaluations. The pilots complained in particular about the uselessness of the retractable landing gear, whose presence did not justify the increase in the aircraft's weight. Consequently, by September 1940, Nakajima had built a further 10 preseries aircraft that employed various solutions to resolve these complaints. An overall reduction in weight and the adoption of a wing with a greater surface area fitted with special "combat" high-lift devices (used in particular circumstances, these allowed the aircraft to carry out tight turns, thus increasing its maneuverability in a remarkable way) proved to be decisive modifications. The Nakajima fighter was finally accepted and went into mass production.

The initial variants (the Ki-43-Ia and Ki-43-Ib) differed only in armament and went into service in June 1941, a total of 716 being built in all. However, after a series of initial successes, the strengthening of the Allied forces revealed an overall inadequacy in performance during the aircraft's operative service, and in 1942 Nakajima developed an improved version (the Ki-43-II), which became the major production series. The main differences lay in the adoption of a more powerful engine and a three-blade variable pitch metal propeller that, together with aerodynamic refinements and structural modifications, made the aircraft more competitive compared to the more advanced Allied fighters. The Ki-43-II variant was built in three series (IIa, IIb, and KAI) that incorporated the various modifications developed in the course of production. In 1944, the final version, the Ki-43-III, appeared and was provided with a 1,230 hp Nakajima Ha-115-II engine (or a 1,250 hp Mitsubishi Ha-112), proving to be the most successful of all, although only 10 prototypes were built. Out of a total of 5,919 aircraft that came off the assembly lines, 3,239 were completed by Nakajima, 2,631 by Tachikawa, and 49 by the arsenal of the Japanese army. The aircraft's career came to an end in the desperate suicide missions that occurred during the final months of the war.

color plate

Nakajima Ki-43-II 2nd Chutai 25th Fighter Sentai Imperial Japanese Army Air Force - China 1943-45

Aircraft:	Nakajima Ki-43-IIb
Nation:	Japan
Manufacturer:	Nakajima Hikoki KK
Type:	Fighter
Year:	1942
Engine:	Nakajima Ha-115, 14-cylinder radial, air-cooled, 1,150 hp
Wingspan:	35 ft 7 in (10.50 m)
Length:	29 ft 3 in (8.92 m)
Height:	10 ft 9 in (3.29 m)
Weight:	6,450 lb (2,932 kg) loaded
Maximum speed:	329 mph (530 km/h) at 13,125 ft (4,000 m)
Ceiling:	36,750 ft (11,200 m)
Range:	1,095 miles (1,760 km)
Armament:	2 machine guns; 1,103 lb (500 kg) of bombs
Crew:	1

A Hayabusa belonging to the 25th Sentai stationed in China.

A Hayabusa with the typical markings of home defense.

DE HAVILLAND MOSQUITO Mk.IV

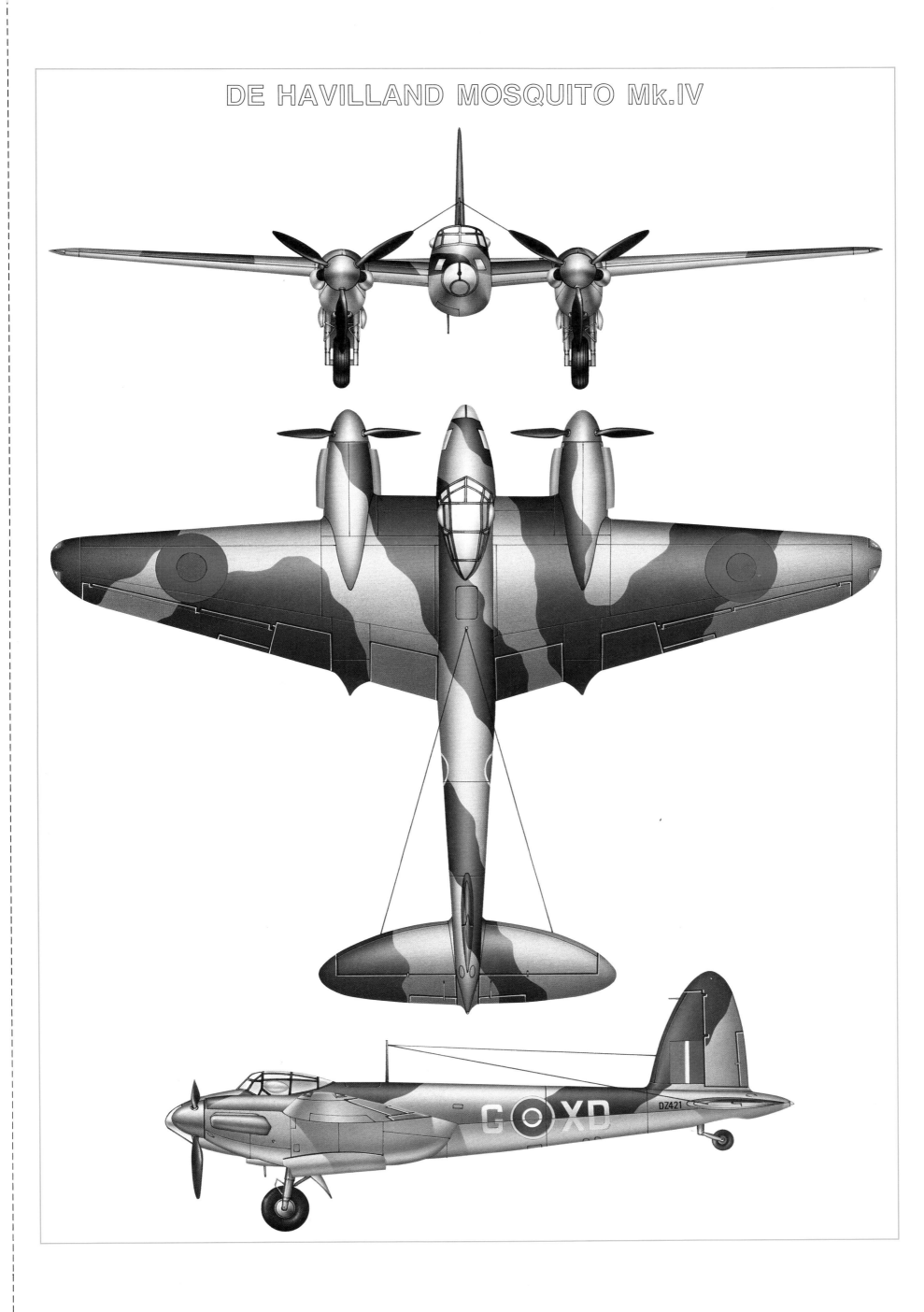

Unanimously recognized as one of the most versatile and effective combat planes built in the course of the war, the de Havilland Mosquito has rightly earned a prominent position among the "immortals" of aviation history. Fighter, reconnaissance plane, bomber: in virtually every role this elegant all-wood two-engine aircraft proved to be remarkable. Its performance was unsurpassable, and it was a deadly weapon, so much so that the final versions remained in service long after the war was over. It was not until 1951 that the units of Bomber Command replaced the old "Mossie" with the twin-jet English Electric Canberra. From 1941 to 1950, no fewer than 6,439 Mosquitos in a dozen variants were built in Great Britain, while a further 1,342 aircraft were constructed in Canada and Australia.

The DH 98 project was launched privately by de Havilland in 1938. The aim was to construct a bomber-reconnaissance plane capable of flying at such a high altitude and at such a great speed that it would not need defensive armament. It was undoubtedly an original beginning, and it was perhaps for this very reason that the project was not initially accepted by the official authorities. It was not until World War II had begun that the Air Ministry began to reconsider de Havilland's proposal, especially since it was planned to build the aircraft entirely in wood, a feature that would have proved invaluable should a shortage of strategic materials have arisen. Work began in great secrecy at the end of December 1939, and just under a year later, on November 25, 1940, the first prototype took to the air.

Right from the start it became apparent that the Mosquito was a "thoroughbred," provided with exceptional maneuverability as well as being extremely fast both in horizontal flight and in ascent (during tests it reached 397 mph - 640 km/h). The key to this success lay in a fortunate combination of several factors: the carefully studied aerodynamic lines; the high weight/power ratio; the pairing of an extremely valid airframe with two equally excellent engines, in this case the Rolls-Royce Merlin. Official skepticism turned to interest, and it was decided to give immediate priority to production. The series of official evaluations began on February 19, 1941, and the first prototype was followed by a second fighter version (on May 15) and by a third reconnaissance version (on June 10). This variant (PA Mk.I) was the first to go into service, in September, as well as to confirm the validity of the theory that had given rise to the project: on September 17, during a daytime reconnaissance mission in France, a Mosquito PA Mk.I easily managed to escape three Messerschmitt Bf.109s that had attacked it by climbing to an altitude of 23,066 ft (7,000 m).

In May 1942 the first Mosquito bomber went into service (241 of this series, the Mk.IV, were built, in two subseries), almost at the same time as the night fighter variant (the Mk.II, of which 467 were built). Many other series were derived from these three initial ones, characterized by constant improvements and up-datings.

A detail showing the position of the Mosquito's armament, concentrated in the nose, and the door by which the crew entered the aircraft.

The reconnaissance versions were almost always derived from bomber variants, the second version of which was the Mk.IX, which appeared in the spring of 1943: it had more powerful engines, and its bomb load was doubled. Toward the end of the same year, the major production series of bombers followed (known as the Mk.XVI, 1,200 were built). These aircraft were provided with a pressurized cockpit, and their bomb load was increased to 3,973 lb (1,800 kg). As for the night fighters, following the construction of 467 Mosquito Mk.IIs, 97 Mk.XIIs and 270 Mk.XIIIs were built from March 1943 and February 1944 respectively.

However, the Mosquito was most widely employed in the role of fighter-bomber. The Mk.VI series was derived directly from the Mk.II adding to the already heavy armament of the fighter two 254 lb (115 kg) bombs in the fuselage and another two beneath the wings; this load was subsequently doubled. This series was the most numerous of all, with a total of 2,584 aircraft being constructed. These Mosquitos went into service in 1943, also being employed by Coastal Command in the role of antishipping attack. They were mainly armed with eight rockets, although a 57 mm cannon was installed for antisubmarine attack. This modification was carried out on 25 aircraft designated Mk.XVIII.

color plate

de Havilland Mosquito Mk.IV 139th Bomber Squadron RAF - Great Britain 1943

Aircraft:	de Havilland Mosquito Mk.IV
Nation:	Great Britain
Manufacturer:	de Havilland Aircraft Co. Ltd.
Type:	Bomber
Year:	1942
Engine:	2 Rolls-Royce Merlin XXI, 12-cylinder V, liquid-cooled, 1,250 hp each
Wingspan:	54 ft 3 in (16.51 m)
Length:	40 ft 10 in (12.42 m)
Height:	15 ft 3 in (4.65 m)
Weight:	21,823 lb (9,886 kg)
Maximum speed:	380 mph (612 km/h) at 21,052 ft (6,400 m)
Ceiling:	31,082 ft (9,449 m)
Range:	1,219 miles (1,963 km)
Armament:	2,002 lb (907 kg) of bombs
Crew:	2

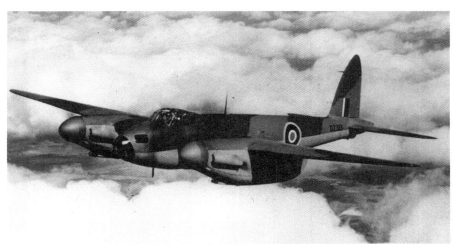

A de Havilland Mosquito in flight. The photo shows the bomber version with glazed nose.

GREAT BRITAIN

Having successfully overcome the first important test of the conflict, the battle of Britain, and having consequently averted the direct threat of a national invasion, Great Britain had the means to consolidate the primary role that it held in the aeronautical field, both at a quantitative and a qualitative level. Thus, the second phase of restrengthening and modernization of the British military aviation began, stimulated not only by the need to face the requests for increasingly competitive aircraft that came from theaters of operation all over the world, but also and above all by the strategical need to attack the enemy directly on its own territory, so as to weaken its almost incredible energy and deprive it of the industrial resources that fed its war machine.

The RAF's most prestigious aircraft were created at this time: the Bristol Beaufighter; the de Havilland Mosquito; the increasingly powerful versions of the Spitfire; the great strategic bombers, the Stirling, the Halifax, and the Lancaster. In fact, it was the entry into action of the second generation bombers, in 1941, that marked the beginning of a new phase in the conflict in Europe. The raids on Germany gradually acquired weight and importance. Initially, only targets of an industrial nature were concerned, but from July 1941 onward, the RAF's Bomber Command was also given the task of damaging the German communications network and weakening the morale of the population, especially those people living in the industrialized areas of the Ruhr and the Rhine Valley. The first carpet bombing raids took place, with heavy use of incendiary bombs, and although the concrete results were not particularly significant, many were carried out: during the year, the amount of bombs released on enemy territory reached 35,000 tons.

In 1942, this type of operation received a decisive impulse with the arrival of the first American units of the 8th USAAF in Great Britain. These gradually backed those of the RAF in bombing missions against the Third Reich. From March onward, techniques were also modified, replacing the waves of aircraft with heavily concentrated bombing on a single, limited target. The first raid of this type was carried out on Lubeck on the night of March 28-29, with almost 300 bombers that released 500 tons of bombs on the city. Similar missions followed on Rostock and, on the night of May 30, the first mass air raid, involving more than 1,000 aircraft, was carried out on Cologne. At the same time, the techniques used to locate targets and to coordinate the enormous number of aircraft were further improved, with devastating results. In the course of 1942, Germany suffered 1,000 attacks, 17 of which were on a large scale with more than 500 tons of bombs being dropped.

It was a massive effort, which was not exhausted until the end of the hostilities, and which was supported perfectly by industrial production. In 1942, no fewer than 23,761 aircraft of all types came off the assembly lines. This was a notable increase compared to previous years, and well represented the progression and intensity of the effort: in 1939, total aeronautical production amounted to 7,000 aircraft; in 1940, this figure increased to 15,000, and in 1941, to a total of 20,100 aircraft in all.

Chronology

1941

January 9. The prototype of the Avro Lancaster, derived from the modified airframe of the two-engine Manchester, makes its maiden flight. This bomber was the most famous of its kind to go into action with the RAF, and, from the end of 1941 to the early months of 1946, a total of 7,366 was built.

February 10-11. The Short Stirling, a four-engine bomber, makes its operational debut in a night raid on Rotterdam. The Stirling was the first in its category to go into service in the units of the RAF, and, although it never achieved the fame of the Halifax and the Lancaster, it served for the entire duration of the war.

May 15. First flight made by a British aircraft powered by a jet engine. This was the Gloster E 28/39 experimental prototype, which, provided with a Whittle W.1 jet engine with 860 lb (390 kg) thrust, was tested successfully. The Gloster Meteor, the first British jet fighter, was to be derived from it.

June 29. The second prototype of the Fairey Barracuda torpedo plane takes to the air; 2,572 aircraft of the definitive configuration of the plane were built in several production series, and they went into service in January 1943 for the rest of the war. Several aircraft remained in the Fleet Air Arm until 1953.

December 22. The prototype of the Fairey Firefly carrier-based fighter makes its maiden flight. The aircraft was employed from October 1943, above all in the Pacific. The final aircraft of the Mk.I series (950 built in all) remained in service until the end of 1946.

1942

February 22. Change at the summit of the RAF's Bomber Command: Air Marshall Arthur Harris is put in command, replacing Air Chief Marshal Sir Richard Peirse. Harris was one of the most fervent supporters of the new "highly concentrated" bombing methods that were adopted in air raids on Germany.

May 30-31. First "thousand bomber" air raid carried out by the RAF on Cologne. In all, 1,046 aircraft were used, with a total of 1,478 tons of bombs being released. This mission was followed shortly after by similar raids on major German cities, including Essen and Bremen.

September 2. The prototype of the Hawker Tempest Mk.V, one of the best fighters used by the RAF during the conflict, takes to the air. It was derived from the Hawker Typhoon and marked a definite improvement. The Tempest went into service in April, 1944, and just over 800 were built. This fast and powerful single-seater distinguished itself in two roles in particular: the pursuit of the German V-1 flying bombs and the interception of the Luftwaffe's Messerschmitt Me.262s, the first jet fighter in service in the world.

AVRO LANCASTER Mk.I

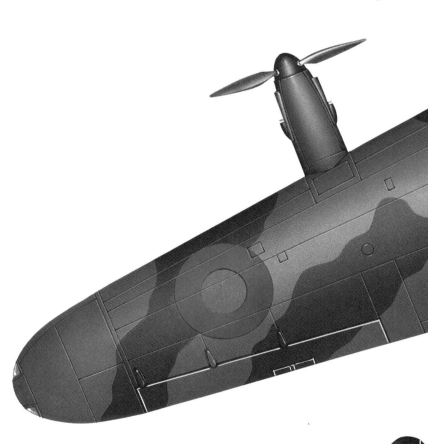

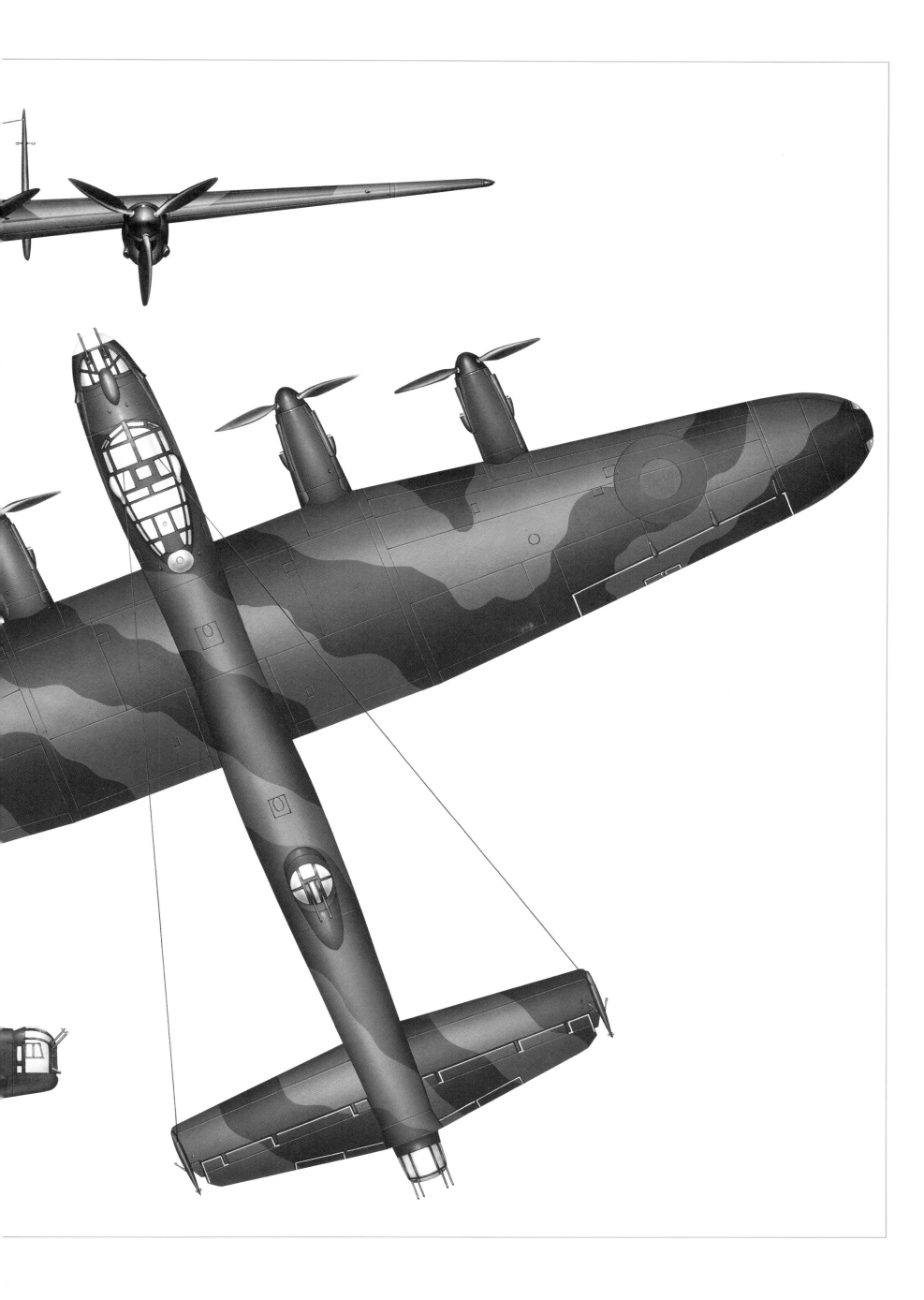

AVRO LANCASTER Mk.I

After the Short Stirling and the Handley Page Halifax, the Lancaster was the last heavy bomber model to go into front-line service with the RAF during the war. However, although it went into service almost a year and a half after its predecessors, the four-engine Avro was clearly superior. Some idea of the importance this aircraft had in the Allied arsenal can be gained from a few figures: from the end of 1941 to the beginning of 1946, a total of 7,366 Lancasters was built; they completed 156,000 missions in the course of the conflict, dropping a total of 608,612 tons of bombs. In comparison, a total of 6,176 Halifaxes was built, and between March 11, 1941 (the date of their first bombing mission), and April 25, 1945, they carried out 75,532 missions, dropping more than 227,000 tons of bombs on European targets.

The specifications that gave rise to the Lancaster were the same as those from which the Halifax project originated in September 1936. The Air Ministry requested the construction of a bomber powered by two Rolls-Royce Vulture engines that were being developed at the time. Avro proposed its model 679 Manchester, which took to the air in the form of a prototype on July 25, 1939, going into production at the end of a series of evaluation tests. The new bomber went into service in November 1940, but right from the start of its operative career the inadequacy of its engines became apparent. They proved to be incapable of providing the aircraft with a performance that could be considered acceptable, especially at altitude. The program seemed destined to fail, considering that Rolls-Royce was too busy with production of the Merlin engine to find time to improve the Vulture, an especially complex power plant. A solution was found in the summer of 1940. This consisted in modifying the Manchester in such a way that it could be fitted with four Merlin engines. Roy Chadwich, the designer, immediately started work on a Manchester taken from the assembly lines, and on January 9, 1941, the new prototype (designated Manchester Mk.III) took to the air. It was followed on May 13 by a second aircraft, and flight tests went beyond even the most optimistic expectations, revealing excellent general characteristics. It was therefore decided to put the four-engine aircraft (officially designated Lancaster Mk.I) into production, replacing the Manchester on the assembly lines as soon as the 200th aircraft had been completed. The first production series Lancaster took to the air on October 31: it differed from the prototype above all in the adoption of more powerful Merlin engines and the installation of turrets on the aircraft's back and in the belly, a considerable increase in weight when fully loaded that also penalized its performance as far as speed was concerned.

Nevertheless, the new bomber was still an excellent aircraft, and production was soon proceeding at a great rate, using assembly lines belonging to other aeronautical manufacturers, such as Austin Motors, Vickers-Armstrong, and Armstrong Whitworth. In all, 3,425 Lancaster Mk.Is were completed, and their operative career (which commenced at the beginning of 1942) was intensive for the entire duration of the conflict. Apart from its excellent flying characteristics and overall performance, the Lancaster's success was also due to its great capacity, which allowed it to carry bombs of increasing size and weight. Many Mk.Is were specially modified to drop bombs weighing over 12,015 lb (5,443 kg), even managing to carry the "Grand Slam," which, at 22,028 lb (9,979 kg), was the heaviest bomb to be carried by an aircraft in the course of the war. The first of these was released on March 14, 1945. Among the numerous missions in which the Lancasters played a leading role, mention should be made of the attack to the Moehne, Eder, and Sorpe dams in the Ruhr Valley on the night of May 16/17, 1943. The four-engine aircraft were modified for the occasion in order to carry the special rotating bombs developed by Barnes Wallis.

The high production rate of the Mk.I soon led to a shortage in Merlin engines, and the need to find alternative engines led to the construction of the next variants, the Mk.II and Mk.III.

---

color plate
Avro Lancaster Mk.I 106th Bomber Squadron RAF - Conningsby, Great Britain 1943

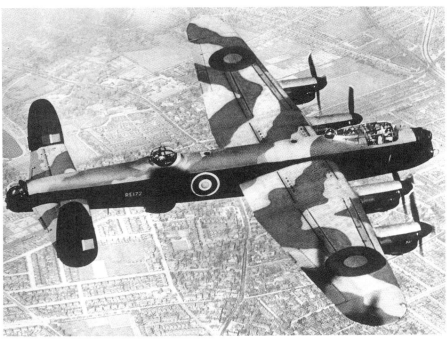

An Avro Lancaster in flight. The aircraft is equipped with an H25 radar beneath the fuselage.

A Lancaster expressly modified for launching the special bombs meant to destroy the dams on the Ruhr. The mission was carried out by the RAF's 617th Bomber Squadron, known as the "Dam Busters".

Aircraft:	Avro Lancaster Mk.I
Nation:	Great Britain
Manufacturer:	A.V. Roe & Co. Ltd.
Type:	Bomber
Year:	1942
Engine:	4 Rolls-Royce Merlin XXIV, 12-cylinder V, liquid-cooled, 1,620 hp each
Wingspan:	102 ft 3 in (31.09 m)
Length:	69 ft 8 in (21.18 m)
Height:	20 ft 0 in (6.10 m)
Weight:	70,092 lb (31,752 kg)
Maximum speed:	286 mph (462 km/h) at 11,513 ft (3,500 m)
Ceiling:	24,671 ft (7,500 m)
Range:	2,527 miles (4,070 km)
Armament:	8 machine guns; 22,046 lb (9,987 kg) of bombs
Crew:	7

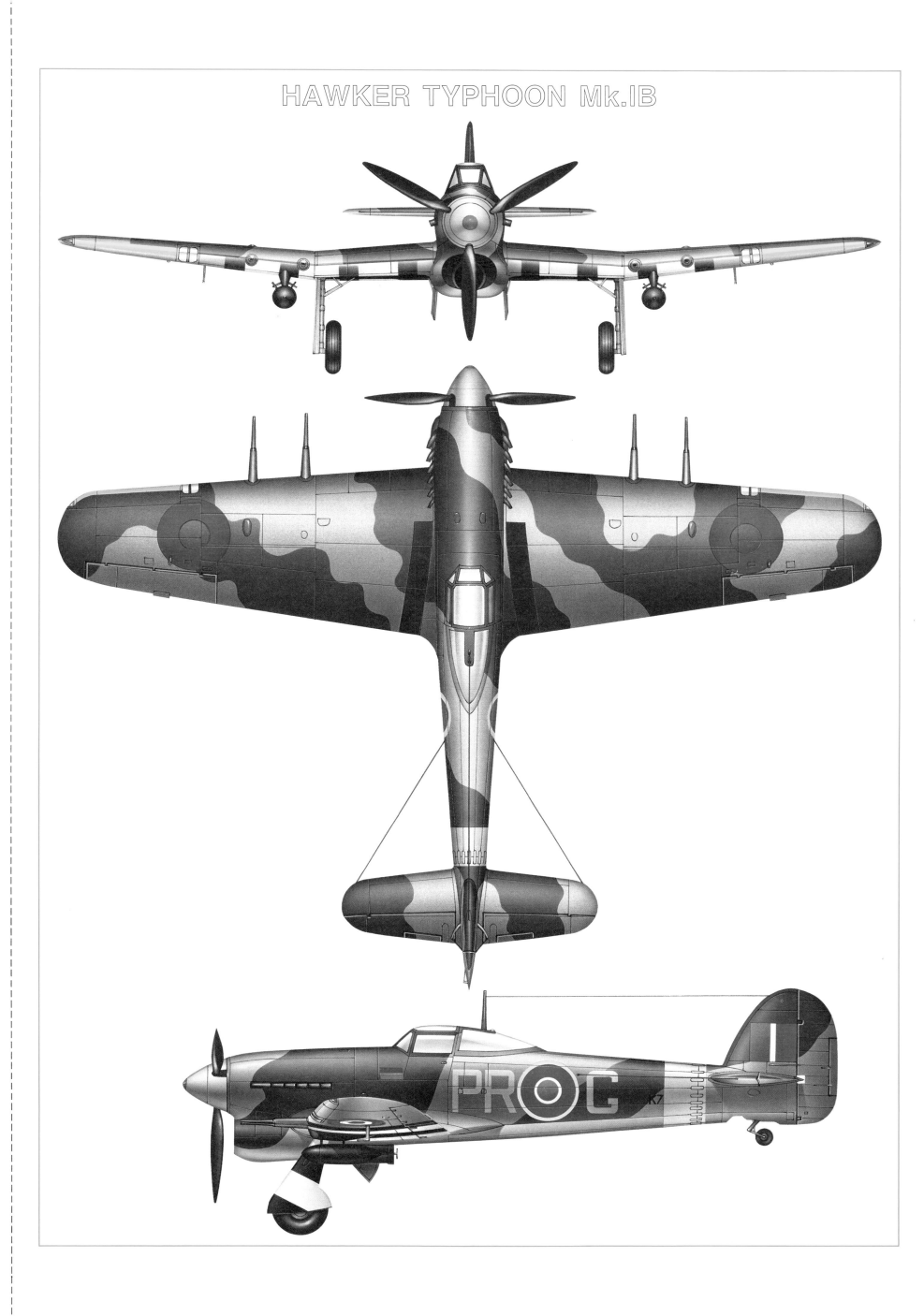

The Hawker Typhoon never succeeded in becoming the powerful interceptor fighter that its designers had intended. However, it did become a formidable tactical support plane, perhaps the most famous to be used in combat by the Allies during the conflict. A total of 3,330 was built in all, and production ceased in 1944.

The specifications that gave rise to the Typhoon were issued by the British Air Ministry in 1937. They called for a fighter powered by the new 2,000 hp engines that were being developed at the time: the Rolls-Royce Vulture and the Napier Sabre. The two engines were very innovative: the former consisted of 24 cylinders arranged in an X formation (in practice, two cylinder blocks from the Peregrine V-12 united on a single base); the latter consisted of 24 cylinders arranged in an H formation (two blocks of 12 horizontal cylinders placed opposite one another, each with its own shaft driving a common reducer). The program was entrusted to the Hawker Company, and Sydney Camm, its chief designer and the "inventor" of the famous Hawker Hurricane, decided to develop four prototypes: two type Rs (known as Tornadoes) with the Vulture engine, and two type Ns (Typhoons) powered by the Sabre.

The first to take to the air was the Tornado, on October 6, 1939, followed by the Typhoon prototype on February 24, 1940. The tests that followed were not particularly successful. There were continuous problems in the functioning of the power plants, as well as by serious structural weaknesses, and the preparatory phase for the two aircraft proved to be extremely long. In 1941, the program for the production of the Vulture engine was abandoned, leaving only the Typhoon in the running. However, even after production had got under way (the first aircraft of the initial Mk.IA series, with armament consisting of 12 machine guns, took to the air on May 27), the fighter continued to be plagued by serious problems that were to last throughout its operative career (deliveries to the RAF units began in September). In fact, the problems concerning weaknesses in the rear section of the fuselage and the functioning of the engines persisted: continuous mechanical breakdowns and an inability to generate the required power clearly demonstrated that the Sabre engine was still far from reaching its definitive stage. The engine's inadequacy was the main reason for the Typhoon's failure as an interceptor, and numerous accidents that led to the loss of many pilots made the Air Ministry begin to seriously consider withdrawing the aircraft from service.

It was not until the second half of 1942 that Hawker entirely managed to solve the problems that plagued the Typhoon. Consequently, having realized the aircraft's limitations and its true capacities, it was decided to use it in the role of ground attack and tactical support and no longer as an interceptor. Thus Sydney Camm's fighter began its "second career," a career that was to be brilliant and intensive for the entire duration of the conflict and in roles that were to prove entirely suited to the Typhoon's characteristics. In fact, the aircraft was extremely fast at low altitudes (in horizontal flight its performance was superior to that of the German Focke Wulf Fw.190 and even to that of the Spitfire), while its heavy armament made it extremely effective against ground targets, especially armored vehicles.

Following the construction of approximately one hundred Mk.IAs, the major production series was the Mk.IB (the prototype made its maiden flight on May 3, 1941) in which the 12 machine guns were replaced by four 20 mm cannons. These Typhoons went into service on August 19, 1942, and their bomb load was gradually increased, until it included eight rockets and a maximum of 2,004 lb (908 kg) of bombs. More powerful versions of the Sabre engines were fitted in the subsequent subseries. The Typhoon scored its greatest successes during the final year of the war, being widely used initially during the Normandy landing and then in the dramatic operations to reconquer Europe.

A formation of Hawker Typhoon Mk.IBs armed with cannons. These aircraft have the old canopy of the earlier model.

A Typhoon Mk.IB, armed with rockets beneath the wings, while taxiing. The aircraft is fitted with the new bubble canopy.

color plate

Hawker Typhoon Mk.IB 609th Squadron RAF - Biggin Hill, Great Britain 1943

Aircraft:	Hawker Typhoon Mk.IB
Nation:	Great Britain
Manufacturer:	Hawker Aircraft Co. Ltd.
Type:	Fighter
Year:	1942
Engine:	Napier Sabre IIa, 24-cylinder H, liquid-cooled, 2,210 hp
Wingspan:	41 ft 8 in (12.67 m)
Length:	32 ft 0 in (9.73 m)
Height:	14 ft 10 in (4.52 m)
Weight:	13,267 lb (6,010 kg)
Maximum speed:	404 mph (652 km/h) at 18,025 ft (5,480 m)
Ceiling:	35,100 ft (10,670 m)
Range:	608 miles (980 km)
Armament:	4 × 20 mm cannon; 2,004 lb (908 kg) of bombs
Crew:	1

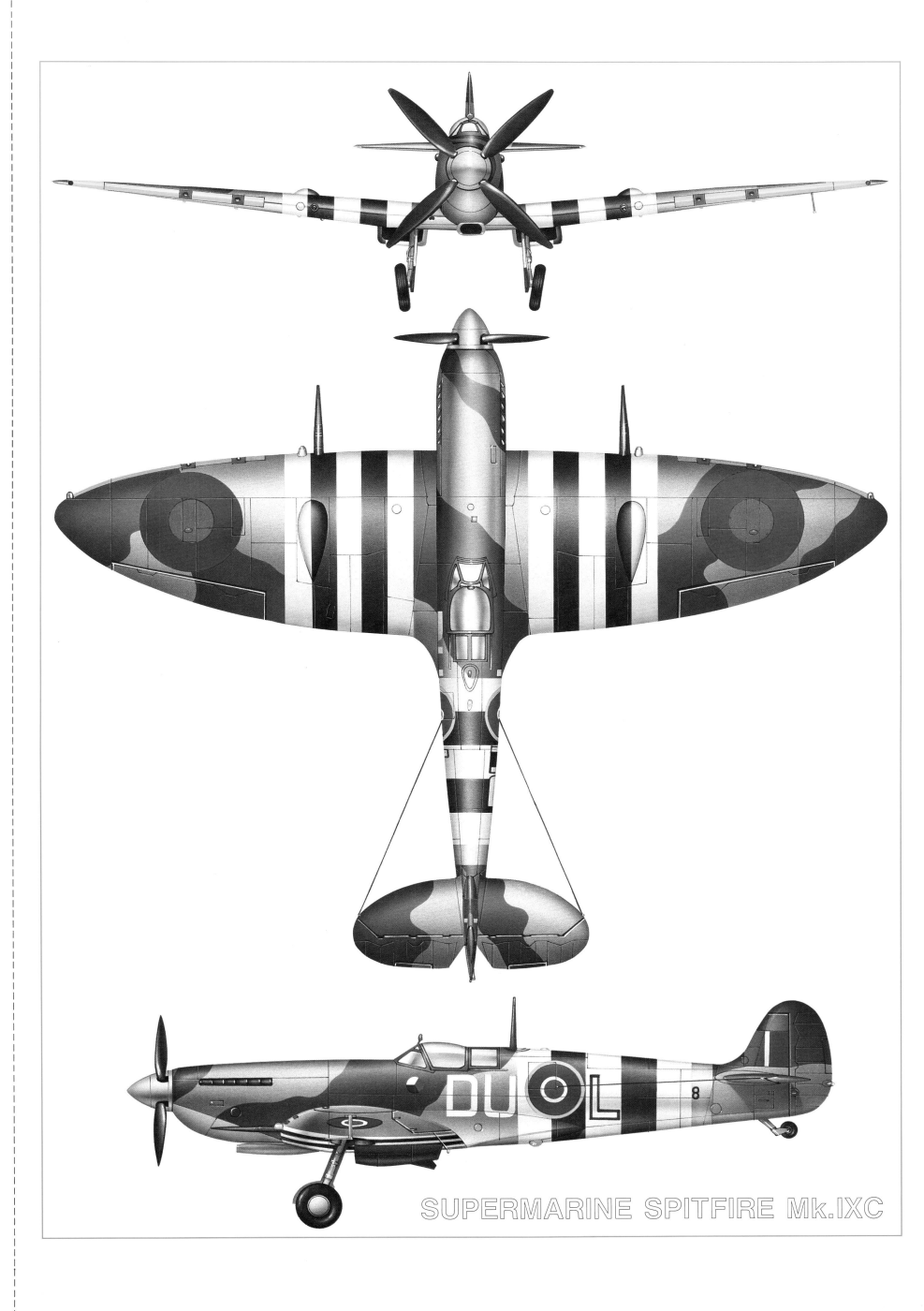

SUPERMARINE SPITFIRE Mk.IXC

Two Spitfire Mk.IXs in flight over Mount Vesuvius, near Naples.

The continuous search for supremacy over the German fighters led, in 1942, to the development of a new variant of the Supermarine Spitfire, the best British fighter of the conflict and among the best of those of all the countries taking part in the war. This version, built specially to contest the superiority of the Focke Wulf Fw.190 over the Spitfire Mk.V, was the Mk.IX, which appeared in July and was basically a combination of the airframe of the Mk.V with a more powerful version of the Merlin engine, generating 1,565 hp. A total of 5,665 Spitfire Mk.IXs was built in all, in numerous subseries. These differed in their employment at low, medium, and high altitude (with wings type LF, F, and HF respectively) and in their armament (type B, C, or E, the latter suffix indicating two 12.7 mm machine guns, two 20 mm cannons, and a bomb load of up to 1,002 lb - 454 kg).

The Spitfire Mk.IX began to reequip the units of the RAF's Fighter Command from July 6, 1942 (the first unit to receive the new fighter was the 64th Squadron), but it was soon widely used. One of the greatest employers of the aircraft, apart from the RAF, was the Soviet Union, which received no fewer than 1,188 Mk.IXs within the context of the military aid program from mid-1944 until April 1945.

Among the numerous variants of the Spitfire Mk.IX, mention should be made of the one designated Mk.XVI (of which 1,054 were built), which differed from the basic model mainly in the adoption of a Merlin engine built on license in the United States by Packard. This decision was taken in 1943 in order to increase production of the Spitfire to a maximum: the engine built in the United States was a Merlin 66, capable of generating 1,705 hp, and when exportation to Great Britain commenced at the beginning of the following year (with the designation Merlin 266), it was installed in the new version of the fighter. The Spitfire Mk.XVI was constructed with armament of type C or type E, and with F or LF type wings. In the final production series the famous canopy was replaced by another "drop-shaped" one, providing the pilot with greater visibility over 360 degrees. This modification made it necessary to alter the rear part of the fuselage, which was lowered.

The evolution of the prolific series of Spitfires continued. Further variants were developed as well as the Mk.IX. These included the Mk.VI and Mk.VII (100 and 140 built respectively) with improvements for interception at high altitudes: the former was fitted with a 1,435 hp Merlin engine and had a pressurized cabin and pointed type HF wings; the latter was fitted with a Merlin 61, 64, or 71 engine with two-stage supercharger, pressurized cabin, retractable tail wheel, and a larger vertical rudder with a characteristically pointed shape. The Spitfire Mk.VIII should also be mentioned. A total of 1,658 was built, and they were provided with Merlin 61, 63, 66, or 70 engines with two-stage supercharger. The Mk.X and Mk.XI series (16 and 471 aircraft built respectively) were constructed for photographic reconnaissance. They were both unarmed, and the former was provided with a pressurized

cabin. In 1943 the Spitfire airframe was substantially improved, with the appearance of the first Mk.XIIs fitted with the new Rolls-Royce Griffon engine. As well as seeing the creation of more powerful and prestigious versions of the Spitfire, the same year also marked the beginning of the second phase of Reginald J. Mitchell's fighter's operative career, which was to continue well into the 1950s.

color plate

Supermarine Spitfire Mk.IXC 312th (Czech) Squadron RAF - Operation Overload, June 1944

Aircraft:	Supermarine Spitfire Mk.IX
Nation:	Great Britain
Manufacturer:	Supermarine Division of Vickers-Armstrong Ltd.
Type:	Fighter
Year:	1942
Engine:	Rolls-Royce Merlin 61, 12-cylinder V, liquid-cooled, 1,565 hp
Wingspan:	36 ft 10 in (11.22 m)
Length:	30 ft 6 in (9.30 m)
Height:	11 ft 5 in (3.48 m)
Weight:	7,500 lb (3,400 kg) loaded
Maximum speed:	408 mph (656 km/h) at 25,000 ft (7,620 m)
Ceiling:	44,000 ft (13,400 m)
Range:	434 miles (700 km)
Armament:	2 × 20 mm cannon; 4 machine guns
Crew:	1

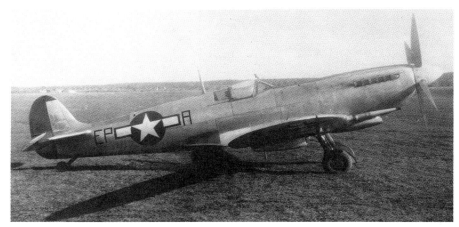

A Spitfire Mk.IX bearing American insignia.

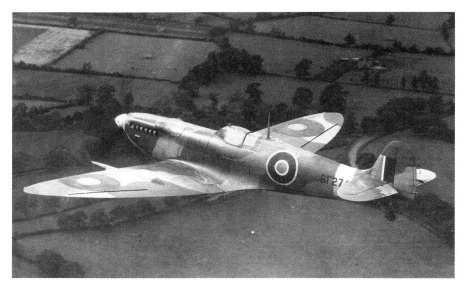

A Spitfire Mk.IX during a test flight. The aircraft bears national insignia but still lacks its unit code.

GERMANY

The myth of the invincibility of the Luftwaffe did not last beyond the first year of the war. However, the first defeat, which occurred in the Battle of Britain, did not reduce the immense potential of the German air force, which was by then involved on fronts that went beyond the borders of Europe, spreading from the Mediterranean to the Balkans and to Russia.

Nevertheless, from 1941, the German aggressor also started to become a victim. German territory became the main objective of an incessant and increasing series of bombing raids, initially carried out by the British RAF, and then also by the American units of the 8th USAAF stationed in Great Britain. Thus, within the space of a year, the roles had been reversed, although with the difference that the power of the Allies was much greater than that which the Luftwaffe had managed to muster during the battle of Britain. From July 1941, the air raids on Germany assumed primary importance in the operative endeavors of the RAF's Bomber Command, with the launching of the first carpet-bombing raids being executed with the dual aim of disrupting the German communications network and of weakening the morale of the population in the industrialized areas of the Ruhr and the Rhine Valley. The following year, with the beginning of combined Anglo-American operations, the initiative passed decidedly into the hands of the Allies as far as air operations in the West were concerned, and the Luftwaffe was forced definitively into a defensive role.

At this turning point in the conflict, accentuated by the unfavorable course of operations for the Axis forces in the main theaters of war, such as East Africa and the Russian front, the institutional limitations that lay at the basis of the formation and employment of the German military aviation emerged once more. The Luftwaffe increasingly proved to be lacking effective strategical power, and this inferiority was particularly stressed by the lack of a heavy four-engine bomber in its arsenal with a performance similar to those that were by then releasing ton after ton of bombs on Germany's cities and factories both night and day. The Heinkel He.177, the only aircraft of this type, began to go into front-line service in 1942, although its employment suffered from the same uncertainties from which it had originated back in 1936, and was always sporadic.

Nevertheless, Germany managed to compensate for this lack by putting a large number of combat planes into production and adapting the principal types already in existence to the change in operative needs with great flexibility. In fact, it was the need for defense against the Allied raids that stimulated the increase in night fighters and the preparation of extremely efficient flying techniques and control of their operations.

The industrial network supported this effort perfectly, right up to the final day of the war. In September 1939, at the time of the invasion of Poland, the German aeronautical industry was already steadily producing 1,000 aircraft a month, for an air force that had 4,840 of the most advanced and competitive front-line aircraft at its disposal, including 1,750 bombers and 1,200 fighters. In 1939 alone, no fewer than 8,300 aircraft of all types were completed. The following year this figure increased to 10,800, reaching 11,800 in 1941, and 15,000 aircraft of all types in 1942.

Chronology

1941

May 20. The Luftwaffe organizes the greatest air raid ever carried out up till then. Known as Operation Merkur, its objective was the invasion of Crete. Approximately 650 aircraft were sent into action to provide air cover for the paratroops, 80 or so gliders, and almost 700 three-engined Junkers Ju.52s used to transport the paratroops or tow the gliders. The operation was a success, although at a high price in terms of men and aircraft.

September 14. The giant Messerschmitt Me.321 attack gliders are used in action for the first time during a mission on the island of Saaremaa in the Baltic. However, these aircraft proved to be very difficult to tow and were replaced by the Me.323s, fitted with four engines capable of guaranteeing flight at altitude after a towed takeoff.

October 2. The third prototype of the Messerschmitt Me.163 rocket interceptor, piloted by Heini Dittmar, reaches 623 mph (1,004 km/h) in horizontal flight. This aircraft, the only one of its kind and the first to be powered by a rocket engine, became operative on May 13, 1944, and just under 300 were built. Christened *Komet*, the Me.163 was used above all against the huge formations of Allied bombers.

1942

July 18. The third prototype of the Messerschmitt Me.262 makes its maiden flight. It was the definitive configuration (as far as its engines were concerned) of the world's first jet fighter. The historical event took place at Leipheim airport, and the aircraft was piloted by Fritz Wendel. Exactly a year later (July 23, 1943), following an intensive series of evaluations, the aircraft was presented to Goering and, on November 26, to Hitler. However, production suffered serious delays, and it was not until the spring of 1944 that the first aircraft reached the units. In all, 1,430 of the revolutionary combat plane were built.

October 3. First successful launch, in the town of Peenemunde, of the A-4 German ballistic missile. Better known by the name of V-2, it was the final improvement to all the work carried out until then by Wernher von Braun. It was a completely controllable machine, weighed almost 13 tons at launching, and had a speed of 5,215 feet (1,585 m) per second at the moment its engine cut out. It had an apogee of 60 miles (96 km).

November 15. The prototype of the Heinkel He.219 night fighter, the first to be built as such for the Luftwaffe, makes its maiden flight. This fast and efficient two-engine aircraft proved to be the best of its kind to be sent into action by Germany, although just under 300 reached the units. It was also the first aircraft in the Luftwaffe to have retractable forward tricycle landing gear and the first in the world to be provided with ejecting seats for the crew.

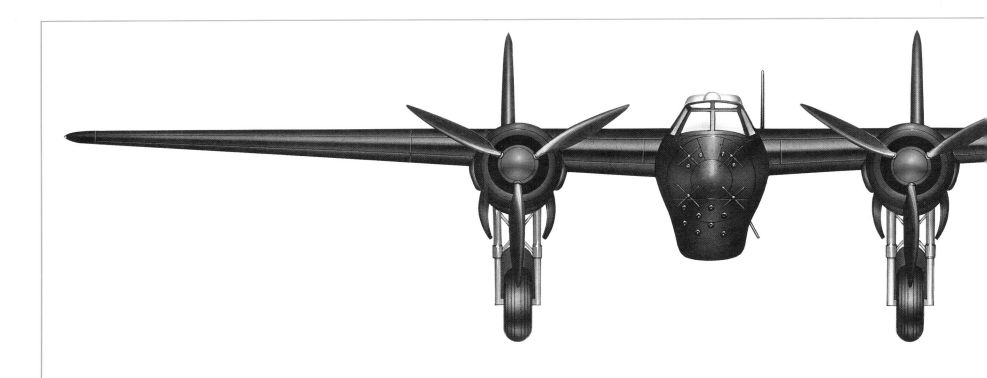

DORNIER Do.217 J-2

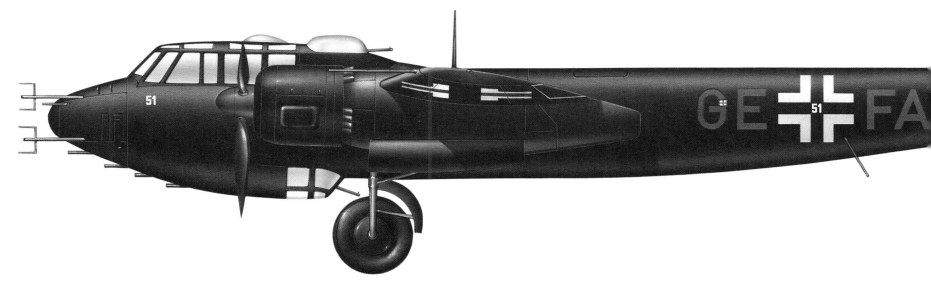

In 1938, the prolific family of two-engine Dorniers that had originated with the Dornier Do.17 in the early 1930s was enriched by the addition of a new variant (the Do.217), which embodied the potential of the original project to the full and which eventually made its mark mainly due to its great versatility. In fact, the approximately 1,905 aircraft built in the period between June 1940 and June 1944 were successfully employed as bombers, reconnaissance planes, torpedo planes, and night fighters.

Following the initial production series, the Do.217 A, which was for reconnaissance (only eight were built, and they went into service in 1940), and the subsequent series, the Do.217 E (which went into service as a bomber in the spring of 1941), the development of the bomber versions went ahead at the same time as that of the night fighter variants. The former included the Do.217 K, which appeared during 1942 and was characterized by a modified nose and heavier armament consisting of eight machine guns for defense and a bomb load of up to 8,830 lb (4,000 kg). In the same year, the Do.217 M also appeared and was provided with 1,750 hp in-line Daimler Benz DB 603 engines.

Although the Do.217 bombers eventually absorbed most of the overall production (a total of 1,541 was built in several variants), the growing importance of defense against the continuous heavy bombing raids carried out by the Allies on German territory gave a powerful impetus to the construction of the night fighter versions.

The first of these was the Do.217 J, which appeared toward the end of 1941 in the initial J-1 series. The aircraft was derived directly from the E-2 variant, maintaining its overall configuration except for the nose, in which the glazed position for a bombardier was replaced by a ''solid'' housing for the offensive armament. This consisted of four 7.9 mm MG 17 machine guns and four 20 mm MG FF cannons. In addition, there were another two

13 mm MG 131 machine guns, while the bomb hold was retained in order to carry up to 883 lb (400 kg) of bombs. The J-1 series was followed by the J-2 (which was produced in the second half of 1942), similar to the previous version but provided with Liechtenstein radar apparatus in the nose and lacking the central bomb hold.

The second version of the night fighter, the Do.217 N, was derived from the M variant bombers. The prototype of the initial N-1 series appeared halfway through 1942, and although it was similar to its predecessor, the J-2, it was fitted with a pair of Daimler Benz DB 603 A engines, generating 1,750 hp each in place of the BMW 801 radial engines. Its armament consisted of four 7.9 mm MG 17 machine guns, four 20 mm MG 151 cannons, and of four two 13 mm MG 131 weapons for rear defense. Moreover, the bomb hold was once again retained and had a capacity of 883 lb (400 kg) of bombs. In the next series, the N-2 (which went into service in 1943), the radar apparatus was improved, and the two rear MG 131 machine guns were eliminated. In these aircraft it was also possible to mount four 20 mm MG 151 cannons on the back, installed in such a way as to shoot upward at a 70 degree angle. Known as Schräge Musik, these weapons were employed flying below the formations of enemy bombers. In all, about 200 Do.217 N-2s were built, out of a total of 364 night fighters in several variants. However, these two-engine aircraft were not popular with their crews. They remained in service until the early months of 1944.

color plate
Dornier Do.217 J-2 Nachtjagd Luftwaffe - Germany 1943

A Dornier Do.217 J-2 night fighter, fitted with radar.

A Dornier Do.217 M bomber with in-line engines during the evaluations carried out in Great Britain after the war.

Aircraft:	Dornier Do.217 J-2
Nation:	Germany
Manufacturer:	Dornier Werke GmbH
Type:	Night fighter
Year:	1942
Engine:	2 BMW 801D, 14-cylinder radial, air-cooled, 1,580 hp each
Wingspan:	62 ft 6 in (19.00 m)
Length:	62 ft 1 in (18.89 m)
Height:	16 ft 4 in (4.98 m)
Weight:	29,094 lb (13,180 kg)
Maximum speed:	323 mph (520 km/h) at 13,125 ft (4,000 m)
Ceiling:	29,065 ft (9,000 m)
Range:	1,428 miles (2,300 km)
Armament:	4 × 20 mm cannon; 6 machine guns
Crew:	3

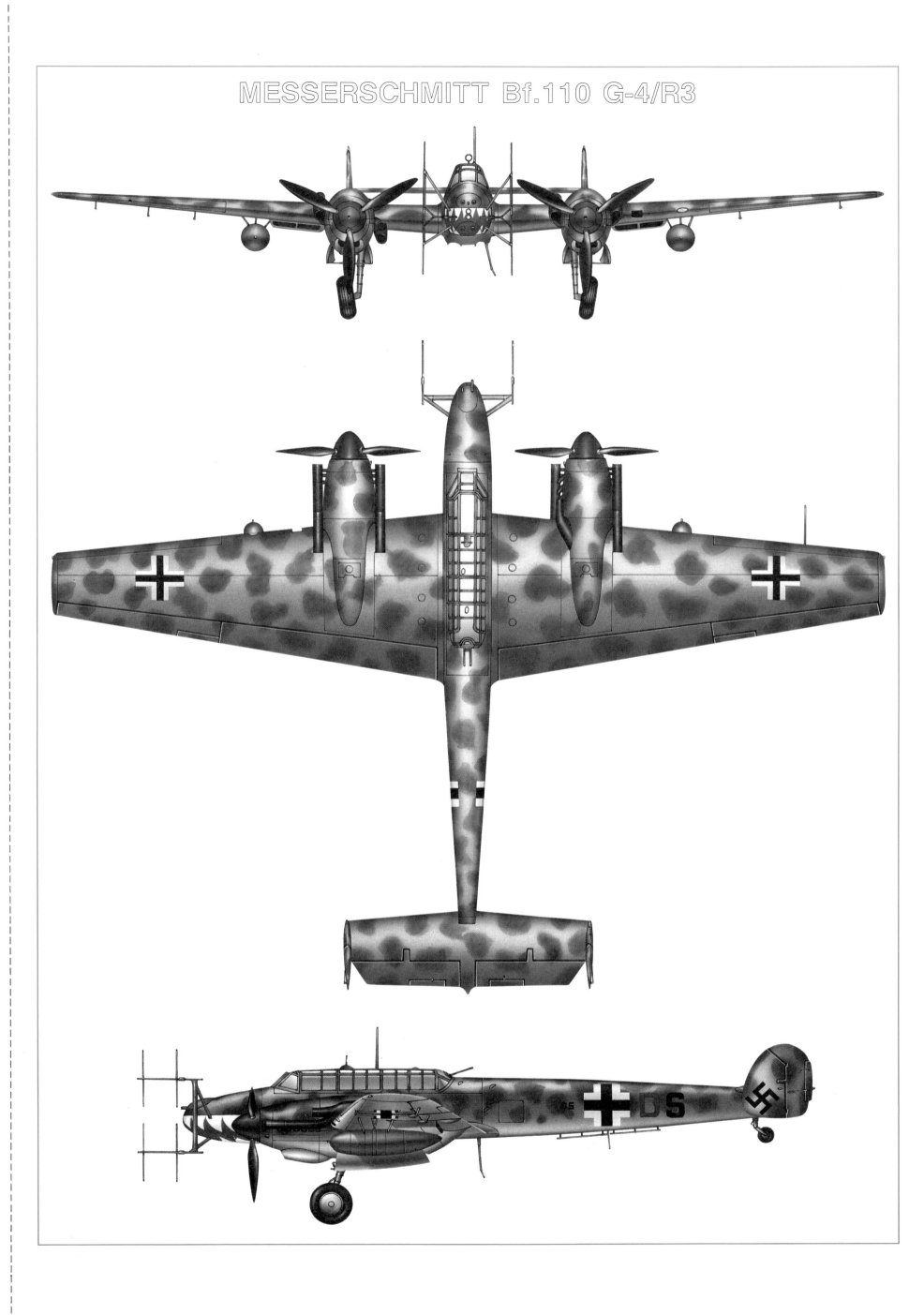

Beyond doubt, the Messerschmitt Bf.110, which was a sensational failure as a heavy fighter, redeemed itself especially in the role of night fighter, in which it served from 1941 until the end of the war. The two-engine Messerschmitts scored considerable success in this speciality, and this success increased with the introduction of Liechtenstein interception radar. Although this apparatus penalized the aircraft's performance because of the large antennae installed on the nose, it contributed to rendering the Bf.110 a particularly effective weapon against the massive raids carried out by Allied bombers on German territory.

The first experiences in this role were carried out by several series of the D and F versions, and in particular by the Bf.110 F-4. These aircraft (which went into production from 1941) were provided with two Daimler Benz DB 601F engines generating 1,350 hp, while the already heavy standard armament, consisting of two 20 mm cannons and four 7.9 mm machine guns, was strengthened in some cases by the addition of two 30 mm cannons in fairings below the fuselage. Radar apparatus was also installed in the next subseries, and despite a decrease in the aircraft's performance due to the increase in overall weight and greater aerodynamic resistence, they scored some notable successes. The fighter was made even more effective against the Allied bomber formations by the installation of two fixed cannons on the aircraft's back positioned to fire upward at a 60 to 70 degree angle (Schräge Musik).

Toward the end of 1941, when it became clear that the program for the Messerschmitt Me.210 (designed as the Bf.110's successor) still had a long way to go, it became necessary to construct a new and more powerful variant of the two-engine aircraft. This was the Bf.110 G, fitted with a pair of 1,475 hp Daimler Benz DB 605 B engines and with substantial improvements from an aerodynamic point of view. The definitive night fighter version, the G-4, was developed from it and went into production in June 1942. Another variant to serve as a night fighter (the H-4) was also derived from the final production version, the Bf.110 H, a small number of which were built from 1942 onward, at the same time as the G version. The differences between the two were minimal and consisted mainly in the H series being fitted with two Daimler-Benz DB 605 E engines and in an overall structural strengthening.

It was these aircraft that bore the brunt of the defense of German territory throughout 1943, and the use of the Bf.110s in this role reached a climax at the beginning of the following year, when 60 percent of the night fighters at the Luftwaffe's disposal consisted of the two-engine Messerschmitts. In all, the front-line reached a maximum of almost 320 of these aircraft. Their operative career was very extensive and was marked by continuous success, due also to the increasingly sophisticated tactics of flying and approach adopted by the units and the ground controllers: between November 18, 1943, and March 31, 1944, RAF Bomber Command's losses amounted to 1,047 aircraft, almost three-quarters of which were victims of the Luftwaffe's night fighters. In fact, on January 21, 1944, no fewer than 55 bombers out of a total of 648 were lost during a raid on Magdeburg, and the same fate awaited a further 43 aircraft a week later during a raid on Berlin. Among the Bf.110 G-4 pilots, the greatest number of victories was scored by Major Heinz-Wolfgang Schnaufer, who shot down 121 planes. In second place was Major Helmut Lent, with a total of 102.

Detail of the antenna of the Liechtenstein SN2 radar. The small antenna in the center of the nose is that of the Liechtenstein C1 radar.

A Bf.110 G-4 that was captured and evaluated in Great Britain after the war. The aircraft is provided with radar and supplementary fuel tanks.

color plate

Messerschmitt Bf.110 G-4/R3 8th Staffel 3rd Nachtjagdgeschwader Luftwaffe - Belgium 1944

Aircraft:	Messerschmitt Bf.110 G-4
Nation:	Germany
Manufacturer:	Messerschmitt A.G.
Type:	Night fighter
Year:	1942
Engine:	2 Daimler Benz DB 605 B, 12-cylinder in-line, liquid-cooled, 1,475 hp each
Wingspan:	53 ft 5 in (16.25 m)
Length:	41 ft 7 in (12.65 m)
Height:	13 ft 1 in (3.99 m)
Weight:	20,728 lb (9,390 kg)
Maximum speed:	341 mph (550 km/h) at 22,998 ft (7,010 m)
Ceiling:	26,069 ft (7,925 m)
Range:	1,309 miles (2,100 km)
Armament:	2 × 30 mm cannon; 2-4 × 20 mm cannon; 2 machine guns; 1,540 lb (698 kg) of bombs
Crew:	2-3

JUNKERS Ju.87 G

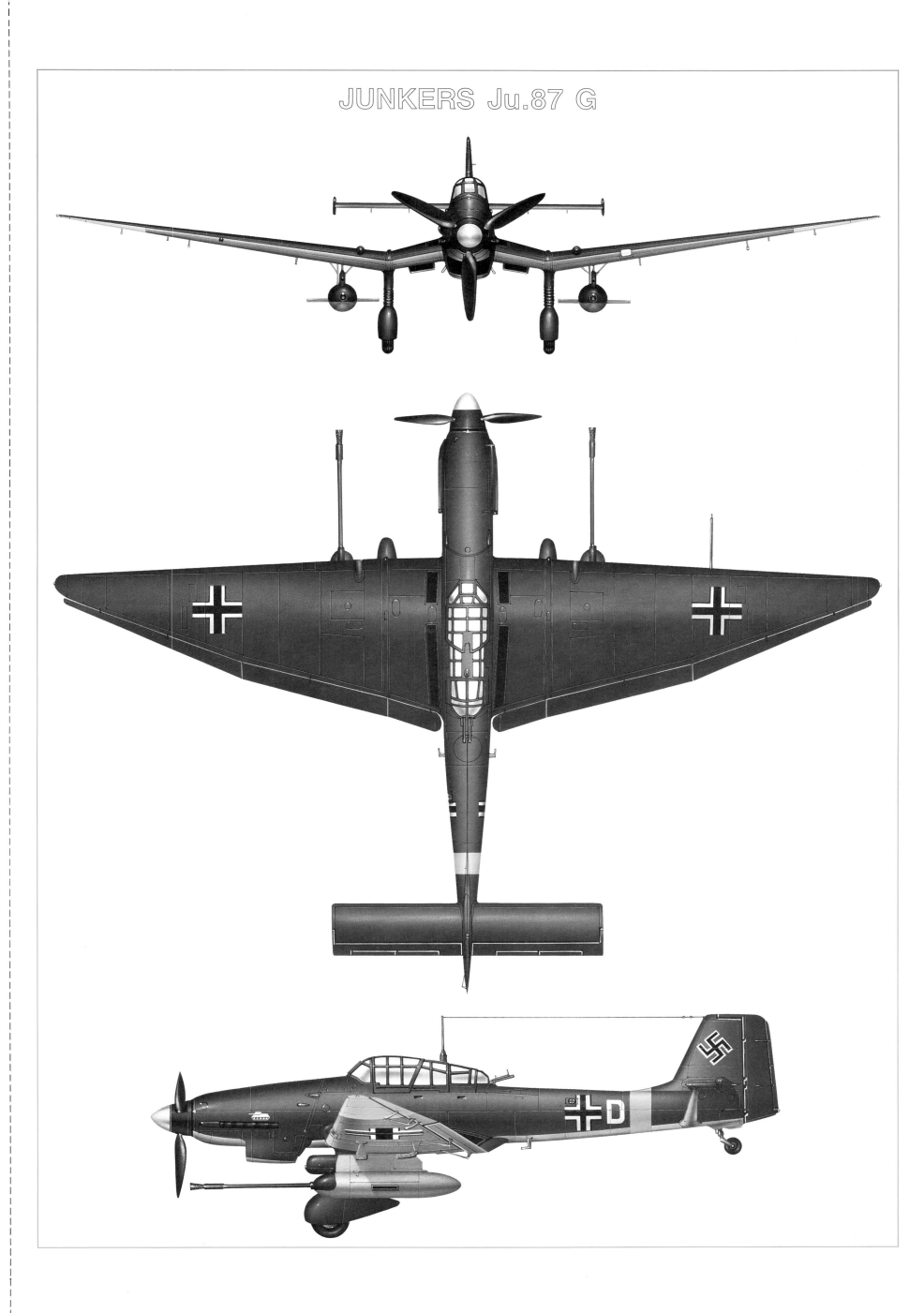

The *Stuka-Kanone*, a Junkers Ju.87 D armed with two cannons below the wings, intended to operate in the intercepting of flying tanks.

Despite the fact that it had been designed in 1933, the Junkers Ju.87 Stuka was one of the most active combat planes to be built in Germany during the conflict. The Stuka remained in production until 1944, a total of more than 5,700 being constructed in all, and it was virtually irreplaceable. In fact, despite numerous projects drawn up with the aim of substituting it, the aircraft remained in front-line service on all fronts until the last day of the war, even after the myth surrounding it as a war machine had greatly declined. Following the initial A and B variants, the most widely used was the D, which appeared in 1941 and represented the maximum development of the airframe.

Compared to its predecessors, the overall performance of the Ju.87 D was remarkably improved (thanks to the adoption of a more powerful Junkers Jumo engine and more carefully studied aerodynamics). It also had better defense (with four machine guns and increased protection for the crew) and was better armed, with the bomb load being increased to 3,973 lb (1,800 kg). The first series (Ju.87 D-1) began to equip the Luftwaffe units in the spring of 1941 and was gradually joined by other subseries that differed from one another mainly in their armament and the power of their engines. The most widely used of these was the D-3, built for ground attack and provided with better armor. A variant specialized in night missions (the D-7) was derived both from it and the subsequent Ju.87 D-5 and was powered by a 1,500 hp Jumo 211P engine. Moreover, 20 mm cannons replaced the machine guns situated on the wings.

It was difficult to find a role for which the Stuka had not been widely tested. Nevertheless, in 1942, the need for an effective antitank weapon led to the construction of a new version, specialized in this very role. This was the Ju.87 G, the last of the long series to go into service and characterized by the installation of two 37 mm BK 3.7 cannons beneath the wings.

The idea of strengthening the offensive armament to a maximum was not new, although up till then all attempts at this had not proved to be a great success in Germany (as, for example, in the case of the Henschel Hs.129). However, in the case of the Ju.87, the result proved without a doubt to be better: although the overall weight of the aircraft increased remarkably, thus affecting its performance (especially as far as speed, altitude, and range were concerned), it proved to be particularly effective. The 37 mm cannon was already used in antiaircraft attack on the ground, weighed 801 lb (363 kg), and was fed by six-shot loaders. It was a deadly weapon in antitank attack, thanks above all to its great initial firing speed, which was more than 2,796 ft (850 m) per second. The Junkers Ju.87 G-1 (the only series to be built) was obtained by modifying the D-5 airframe, on which the experimental installa-

tion was successfully tested in the summer of 1942. These aircraft were employed almost exclusively in Russia and on the eastern front, and it was at the controls of these aircraft that Hans Ulrich Rudel scored his remarkable record, unique among all the pilots who took part in the war: no fewer than 519 Soviet tanks destroyed during 2,530 combat missions, in the course of which he was shot down no fewer than 30 times.

In order to complete the long production of the Ju.87, mention should also be made of another variant that derived directly from the D version.

This was the H, destined for training and built with the aim of speeding up to a maximum the preparation of fighter and bomber pilots in order to replace the heavy losses suffered by the units on the eastern front. Five subseries of the Ju.87 H were built, and the aircraft differed from its predecessors solely due to the presence of dual controls, lack of armament, and a modification to the rear part of the canopy in order to improve the instructor's visibility.

---

color plate

Junkers Ju.87 G 10 (Pz)/SG1 Luftwaffe - Eastern front 1944

Aircraft:	Junkers Ju.87 G-1
Nation:	Germany
Manufacturer:	Junkers Flugzeug und Motorenwerke AG
Type:	Attack
Year:	1942
Engine:	Junkers Jumo 211J, 12-cylinder V, liquid-cooled, 1,400 hp
Wingspan:	49 ft 3 in (15.00 m)
Length:	37 ft 9 in (11.50 m)
Height:	12 ft 9 in (3.90 m)
Weight:	14,569 lb (6,600 kg)
Maximum speed:	195 mph (314 km/h)
Range:	198 miles (320 km)
Armament:	2×37 mm cannon; 1 machine gun
Crew:	2

A Ju.87 D in service with the *Regia Aeronautica*, photographed at an airport in Sardinia in the spring of 1943.

PEARL HARBOR

Little more than an hour. This was the duration of the Japanese attack on Pearl Harbor on the morning of December 7, 1941. In this brief space of time, the 353 aircraft that had taken off from six aircraft carriers cruising at a distance of about 250 miles away inflicted the most crushing blow on the United States forces that they had ever received: 188 aircraft destroyed, a further 159 damaged, 18 ships sunk or seriously hit, 2,403 dead, and 1,778 wounded. From a strategic point of view, the result was even more dramatic: with all its battleships virtually destroyed, the American fleet in the Pacific was left without its most important vessels just when they were most needed. This situation continued for several months and slowed down even further the full launching of operations to counter the strength of an enemy that appeared to be increasingly invincible.

Much has been written and said about Pearl Harbor, about its political and military antecedents, and about its significance in the context of World War II. However, it is worth remembering at least the basic events of this episode in history, if only to underline the fundamental role played by aviation and by carrier-based aviation in particular. Both adversaries, even if from opposing points of view, had means to verify the great potential of the modern aircraft and its enormous strategical importance, expressed for the first time in a theater of operations that was not based on land. For the Japanese, the victory at Pearl Harbor represented confirmation of the military theories that had been put into practice since the phase of rearmament and preparation for the conflict; for the Americans this first defeat represented a strong stimulus, both to continue with the process of modernizing aviation and to accelerate the growth of its strictly military potential.

The value of the natural port of Pearl Harbor, on the island of Oahu in the Hawaii islands, had long been recognized by the United States. A naval base had been set up there since the beginning of the century, and its importance had increased with the passing of the years. This military outpost in the middle of the Pacific was the objective chosen by the Japanese Admiral Isoroku Yamamoto to deliver the first attack of the war. The neutralization of the American fleet was the fundamental premise to the success of the vast air-sea and amphibian operations planned against Malaysia, Siam, the Philippines, and Hong Kong. Yamamoto's plan was presented to the general staff of the navy in the summer of 1941 and was approved, although only after much resistance.

Preparations were careful and intensive, not only as far as the men who were to take part in the action were concerned, but also with regard to the transport and armament that were to be used. For example, because of the shallow depths of Pearl Harbor, the ordinary torpedoes were modified with the adoption of special wooden empennages, while high potential perforating bombs were obtained from 356 mm grenades belonging to the cannons of the navy.

The great naval formation set sail at the beginning of November from several ports and followed different routes, with the aim of not drawing attention to the huge fleet of ships. It was composed of 31 vessels, including the six aircraft carriers (*Akagi, Kaga, Hiryu, Soryu, Zuikaku,* and *Shokaku*) that constituted its main strength. They carried 392 aircraft on board, comprising Mitsubishi A6M2 fighters, Aichi D3A1 dive-bombers, and Nakajima B5N2 high altitude torpedo planes. The command of the fleet was entrusted to Admiral Chuichi Nagumo.

On November 22, the fleet gathered in the Bay of Tankan, in the remote Kurils islands. On November 25 the order to set sail arrived, and the next day the voyage toward Hawaii commenced. On December 2, Admiral Yamamoto gave the final go-ahead for the operation (with a coded message that read "Climb Mount Niitaka"), and five days later, at three o'clock on the morning of December 7, the fleet was in position, heading for Oahu, about 250 miles away. At exactly six o'clock, saluted by the historic battle flag that Admiral Togo had used at Tsushima in 1905, the first aircraft of the attack wave, piloted by Commander Mitsuo Fuchida, took off from the *Akagi* followed within fifteen minutes by the other 182 aircraft. The first formation was composed of 49 B5N2s armed with bombs, by a further 40 of the torpedo version, by 51 dive-bombers, and 43 escort fighters. At 7.15 A.M. it was the turn of the second wave, consisting of 170 aircraft (54 bombers, 80 dive-bombers, and 36 fighters) commanded by Lieutenant Commander Shigekazu Shimakazi. The target of the torpedo planes was the ships at anchor in the main port of Pearl Harbor; the other aircraft were to attack the airports of Wheeler, Hickam, Ewa, Kanehoe, and Fort Island.

At 7.02 A.M. the first Japanese formation appeared on U.S.Army radar installed at Opana, but the alarm, for a series of reasons, was not given in time. At 7.48 A.M. Commander Fuchida launched the first positive signal ("To, To, To", which means "struggle" in Japanese), several minutes after the order to attack ("Tora! Tora! Tora!"). At 7.55 A.M. the first bombs fell on Pearl Harbor, taking it completely by surprise,and the raids had a devastating effect. The torpedoes struck the battleships *West Virginia, Arizona, Oklahoma, Nevada,* and *Utah,* and the cruisers *Helena* and *Raleigh,* while the battleships *California, Maryland,* and *Tennessee* and the support ship *Vestal* were hit by the bombers. The latter also caused damage to the battleship *Pennsylvania,* the cruiser *Honolulu,* and the torpedo-boat destroyers *Cassin, Downes,* and *Shaw.* Fuchida's aircraft also struck the planes parked neatly on the various airfields, and this task was completed by the second wave of the attack, which carried out its mission in an equally deadly and efficient way. At 9.30 A.M. the operation could be considered concluded, and the formations returned to their respective awaiting aircraft carriers, which had come to within 190 miles of Oahu in the meantime. In all, the Japanese had lost barely 29 aircraft (some of these during deck-landing maneuvers) and five midget submarines: a total of 64 men either dead or missing, plus one prisoner, an extremely low percentage compared to the heavy damage inflicted on the enemy. In fact, the final American count was very heavy: the *Oklahoma, Arizona, Utah* and mine-layer *Oglala* were all sunk; heavily damaged, although not sunk, were the *California, West Virginia, Pennsylvania, Tennessee, Maryland, Nevada,* as well as the cruisers *Helena, Raleigh, Honolulu,* the torpedo-boat destroyers *Cassin, Downes,* and *Shaw* and the support ships *Vestal* and *Curtiss.*

Yamamoto's success was therefore great, although not total. In fact, through a series of lucky coincidences, the *Lexington,* and the *Enterprise,* two of the three aircraft carriers in service with the American fleet in the Pacific, escaped the Japanese attack. By chance they were both at sea, the first at Midway, and the second heading for Wake island. Together with the *Saratoga,* these three ships constituted the only advance point of the fleet for many months and the nucleus of an air-sea power that was to increase continuously until the final victory.

HEINKEL He.177 A-5/R6

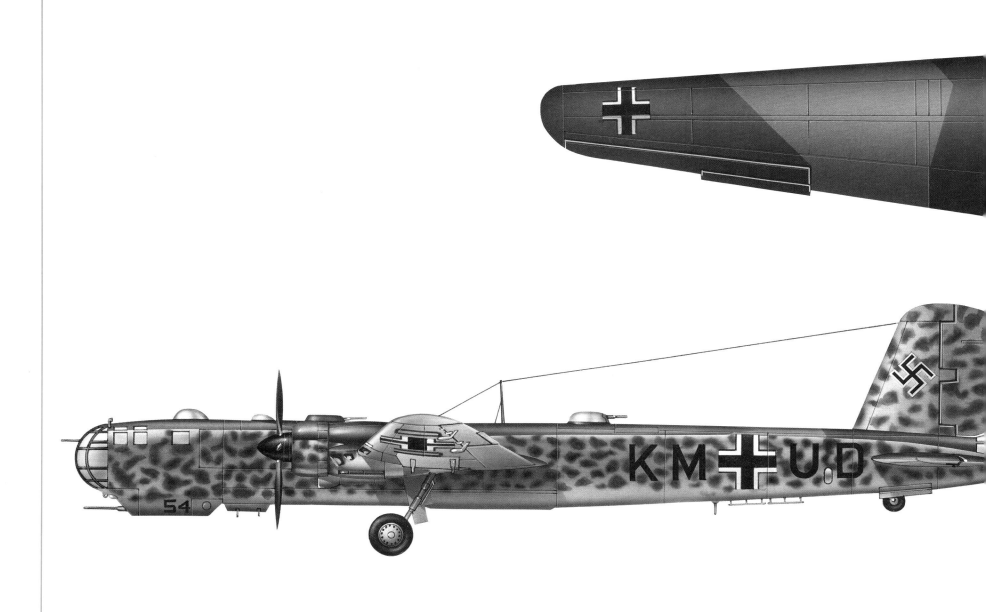

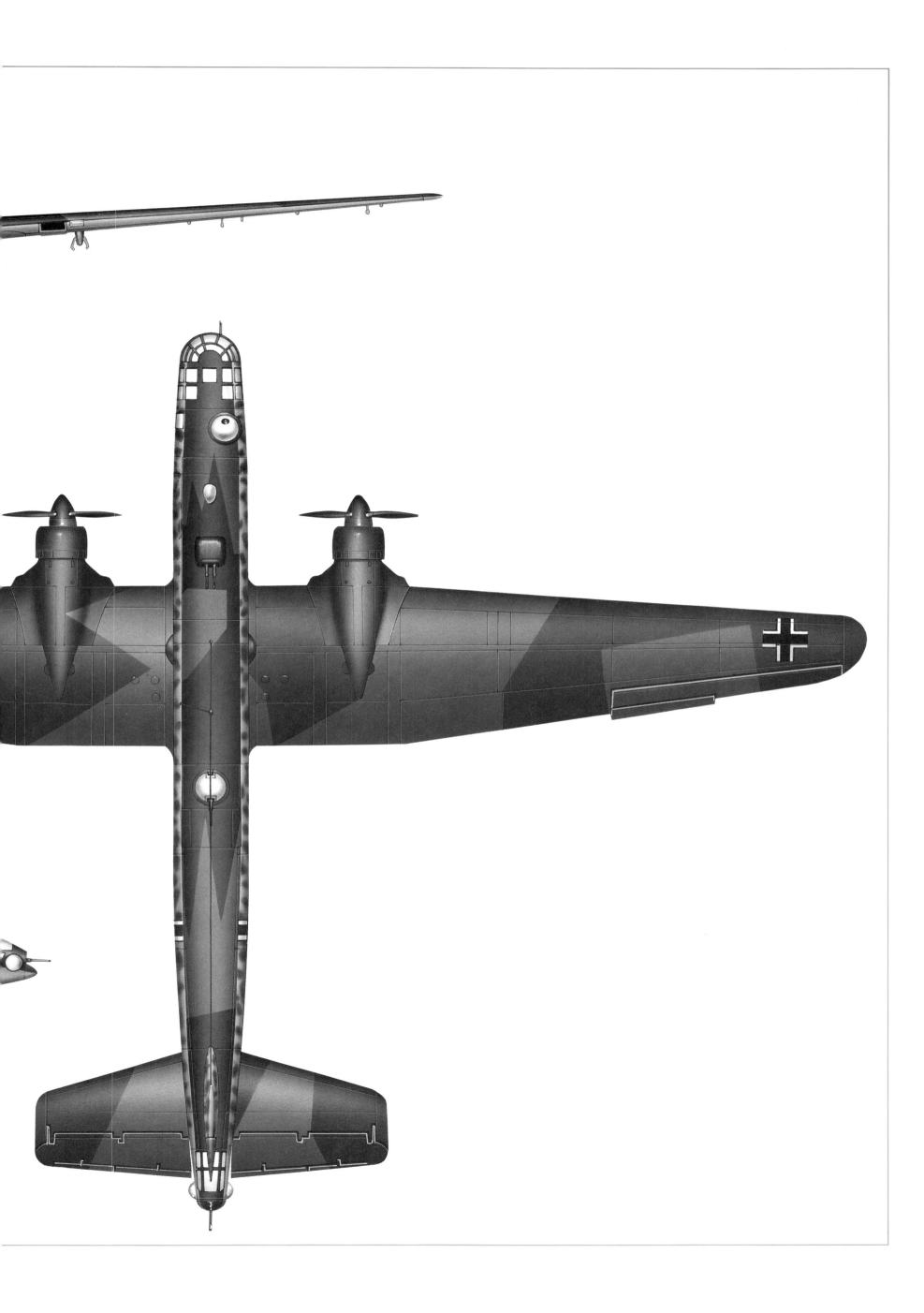

Germany's only attempt to put a heavy bomber into action resulted in a virtual failure. This aircraft was the Heinkel He.177 *Greif*, a large, powerful, and sophisticated plane created to carry out a multitude of tasks including that of dive-bomber, an unusual role for an aircraft weighing 30 tons. Moreover, although it was designed in 1936, the *Greif* did not go into production until six years later, following a long laborious and tormented preparation phase that never succeeded in solving all the problems that plagued the aircraft: structural weaknesses and unreliability of the power plants. Of the approximately 1,000 aircraft that were built, only a few hundred actually went into service, during the final years of the conflict, and even then on an irregular basis.

The specifications that gave rise to Heinkel's P 1041 project, issued in 1936, called for the construction of a long-range strategic bomber, capable of carrying two tons of bombs for 993 miles (1,600 km) and of flying at a maximum speed of 335 mph (540 km/h). These characteristics were undoubtedly exceptional for the time and greatly influenced the project, which was entrusted to Siegfried Günther.

The greatest problem was caused by the engines. In order to reduce the aircraft's air resistance, the designer decided to install only two engines instead of four. Since no 2,000 hp engines were available, the problem was solved by pairing two Daimler Benz DB 601 engines on a single axis, creating the DB 606, which could generate 2,700 hp. This power plant eventually proved to be very complicated and difficult to tune, and it was subject to overheating, which often even caused fires to break out. Things were further complicated by a fresh request from the official authorities, specifying that the He.177 also be capable of carrying out dive-bombing attacks. This meant a series of structural reinforcements, which led to an increase in weight and a subsequent decline in performance.

The first of the five prototypes took to the air on November 19, 1939. The He.177 was a large all-metal two-engine aircraft with cantilever shoulder wing and retractable rear tricycle landing gear. The main landing gear was unusual, with two independent legs on each side, one retracting into the inside of the engine nacelles and the other into their exterior. However, the series of flight tests was not simple. The *Greif* immediately revealed problems in stability and overheating in its power plants, and, subsequently, serious structural weaknesses. Three of the prototypes crashed, and tests continued with 35 preseries aircraft (He.117 A-0) that were built later.

The first production variant was the A-1, of which 130 were built, and deliveries commenced in July 1942. They were followed toward the end of the year by the He.177 A-3 (170 completed), and gradually by the other series, the last of which was the A-5, characterized by numerous modifications to its structure, landing gear, and power plants; 565 were built in all.

In the course of its operative career (which came to a conclusion toward the end of 1944), the He.177 was employed with a great variety of offensive armament. These included the Henschel Hs.293 radio-controlled missiles, which were extremely effective in an antishipping role; the bomber could carry a maximum of three.

color plate

Heinkel He.177 A-5/R6 Kampfgeschwader 40 Luftwaffe - Bordeaux-Mérignac, France 1944

Aircraft:	Heinkel He.177 A-1
Nation:	Germany
Manufacturer:	Ernst Heinkel AG
Type:	Bomber
Year:	1942
Engine:	2 Daimler Benz DB 606, 24-cylinder, liquid-cooled, 2,700 hp each
Wingspan:	103 ft 2 in (31.44 m)
Length:	66 ft 11 in (20.40 m)
Height:	21 ft (6.40 m)
Weight:	66,139 lb (29,960 kg) loaded
Maximum speed:	317 mph (510 km/h) at 19,030 ft (5,800 m)
Ceiling:	22,966 ft (7,000 m)
Range:	745 miles (1,200 km)
Armament:	1 × 20 mm cannon; 5 machine guns; 5,290 lb (2,400 kg) of bombs
Crew:	5

A Heinkel He.177 *Greif* in flight during evaluations carried out by the Allies following Germany's surrender. The aircraft bears British insignia, indicated by black and white stripes.

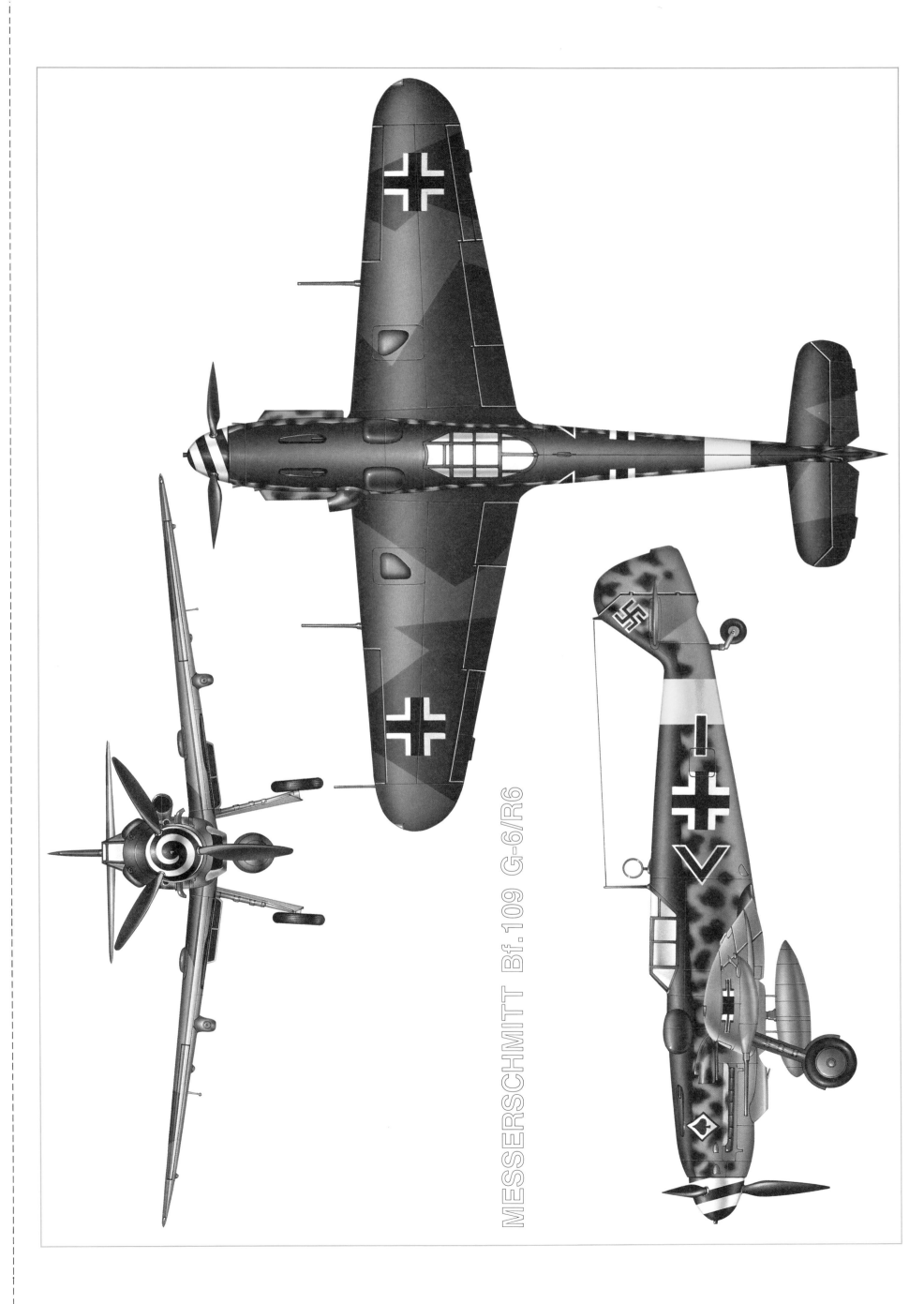

MESSERSCHMITT Bf.109 G-6/R6

A Bf.109 G-6 in flight. The white band on the fuselage indicated the aircraft in service in the Mediterranean.

Like Great Britain's Supermarine Spitfire, Germany's Messerschmitt Bf.109 underwent almost constant improvement. Following the first mass-produced version (the E, which appeared at the beginning of 1939 and was one of the great protagonists of the Battle of Britain), in January 1941 the first aircraft of a notably improved variant, the F, started to go into service. They were considered by many to be the most brilliant aircraft of the series. The main modifications consisted in the adoption of a more powerful Daimler Benz engine and in an overall improvement to the aircraft's aerodynamic characteristics, thanks to the installation of a large spinner in the fuselage, a retractable rear wheel, and the rounding of the wing tips. Moreover, the wings were provided with high lift devices and a different type of aileron.

The first preseries Bf.109 F-0s were tested by the Luftwaffe in the second half of 1940, and after the initial F-1 series had gone into service, mass production went ahead at a great rate with the construction of numerous subvariants, which differed from one another mainly in the type of armament and the engine adopted. Among the most important of these, mention should be made of the F-3 (which appeared at the beginning of 1942) capable of reaching a speed of 389 mph (628 km/h) at an altitude of 22,040 ft (6,700 m); the F-4/B, capable of carrying 1,103 lb (500 kg) of bombs; the F-5 and F-6 (which appeaed toward the end of 1942), which were adapted for the role of fighter-reconnaissance and armed with only two 7.92 mm machine guns. The Bf.109s had a brilliant operative career, especially during the first months in which they were in service, when in some cases the Messerschmitt fighter proved to be superior even to the RAF's Spitfire Mk.V.

It was in fact due to the need to strengthen this superiority (already obtained by the Luftwaffe with the Focke Wulf Fw.190) that the next variant, the Bf.109 G, was built in 1942. This was also the variant of which the greatest number of aircraft was built. The main difference compared to its immediate predecessor lay in the adoption of a Daimler Benz DB 605 engine, capable of generating 1,475 hp. The notable increase in power (the DB 601 installed in the Bf.109 F generated 1,200 hp) allowed for an increase in armament, although this was to the detriment of the aircraft's overall performance.

The first Bf.109 Gs (christened Gustav) went into service in the late summer of 1942, and once again their production was characterized by the construction of numerous series and subseries. Among the most important of these were the G-1, which was provided with a pressurized cockpit and a supercharged DB 605 A-1 engine; the G-2, similar to the previous series but lacking the pressurized cockpit; the G-5, with a DB 605 D engine capable of generating 1,800 hp of power in case of emergency, thanks to a device for water and methyl alcohol, injection as well as a larger rudder; the G-6, whose armament included the installation of a 30 mm Mk.108-type cannon that fired through the propeller hub, two MG 131 machine guns in the nose, and two 20 mm MG 151/20 cannons housed beneath the wings. The final series of Gustavs to go into service was the G-14, provided with external supports for machine guns, rockets, or bombs.

In 1943 the Messerschmitt company began to develop a high altitude version of its fighter. This was the Bf.109 H, which was derived from the F variant and was characterized by a larger wingspan and a Daimler Benz DB 601E engine with a GM-1 supercharging device. The aircraft proved to have a maximum speed of about 465 mph (750 km/h) at an altitude of 33,223 ft (10,100 m), but despite this brilliant performance its development was abandoned following the appearance of serious tail vibrations. However, in the last year of the war the final variant of Messerschmitt's fighter to go into service was derived from the Bf.109 G. In this aircraft, the Bf.109 K, the airframe was developed to a maximum.

color plate

Messerschmitt Bf.109 G-6/R6 II Staffel/JG 53 Jagdeschwader Luftwaffe - Eastern front 1943

A Bf.109 G equipped with *Ofenrohr*, 21 mm rocket launchers installed below the wings and employed against the formations of Allied bombers.

Aircraft:	Messerschmitt Bf.109 G-2
Nation:	Germany
Manufacturer:	Messerschmitt AG
Type:	Fighter
Year:	1942
Engine:	Daimler Benz DB 605 A-1, 12-cylinder V, liquid-cooled, 1,475 hp
Wingspan:	32 ft 6 1/2 in (9.90 m)
Length:	29 ft (8.84 m)
Height:	8 ft 2 1/2 in (2.49 m)
Weight:	6,834 lb (3,095 kg) loaded
Maximum speed:	406 mph (653 km/h) at 28,540 ft (8,700 m)
Ceiling:	39,370 ft (12,000 m)
Range:	528 miles (850 km)
Armament:	1 × 20 mm cannon; 2 machine guns
Crew:	1

A Bf.109 G preparing for takeoff during a mission on the Russian front at the beginning of Operation Barbarossa.

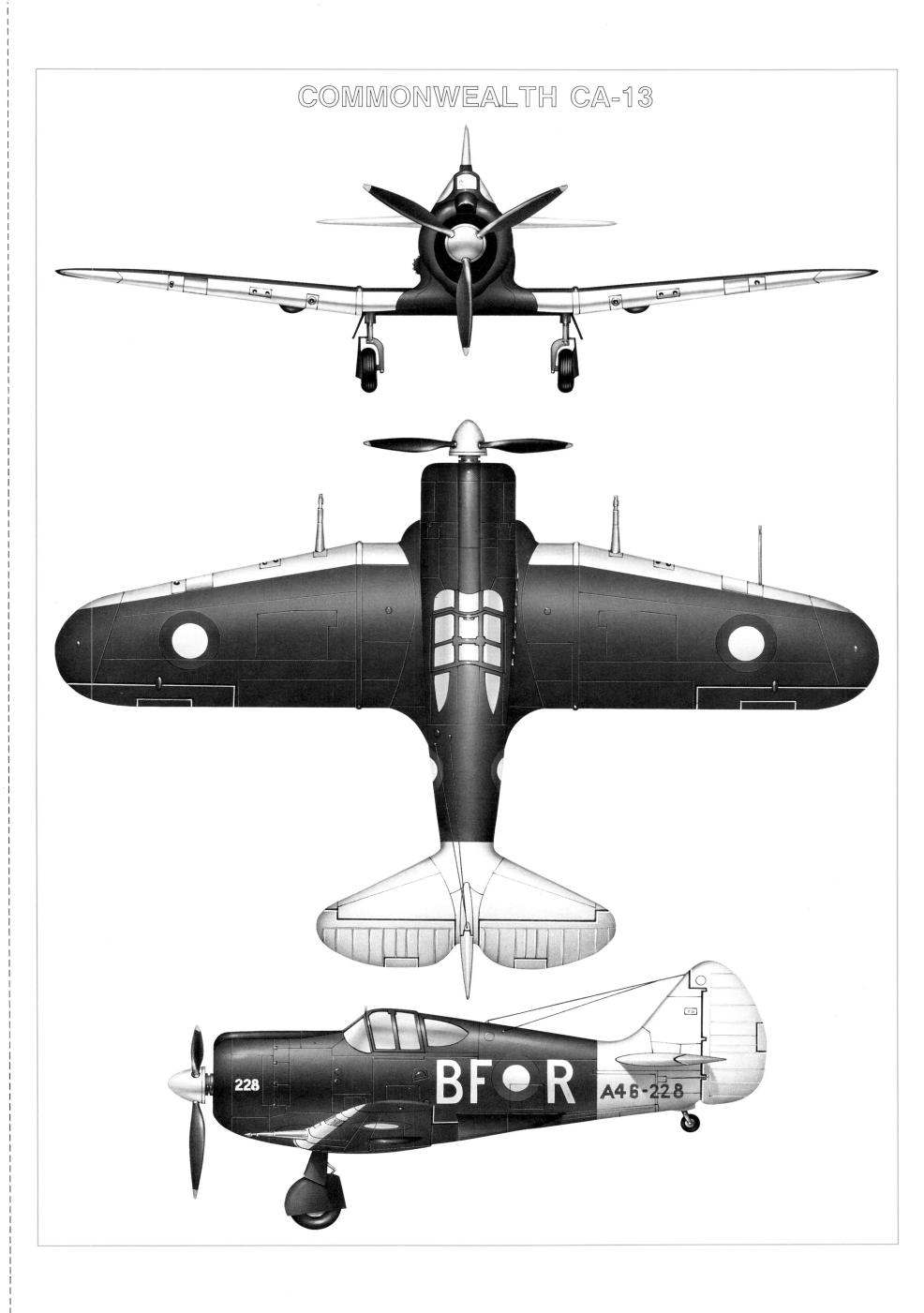

When Japan entered the war, the Royal Australian Air Force was in desperate need of aircraft. At that time, its total strength amounted to only 175 front-line aircraft, most of which were obsolete. The fighter sector consisted of old-fashioned Brewster Buffaloes, which were clearly inadequate compared to their more modern and powerful adversaries. There was a great fear that the country would be invaded, and, faced with the fact that it was impossible for Australia's principal allies (Great Britain and the United States) to provide better equipment within a short space of time, the Australian aeronautical industry decided that it would build a combat plane capable of facing the emergency independently. This was the CA-12 Boomerang, a small, robust, and agile fighter that the Commonwealth Aircraft Corporation (CAC) designed and built within a very brief space of time and that gave invaluable service from 1943 onward, proving to be unbeatable in a tactical role.

The Boomerang, the only entirely Australian-designed aircraft to see combat during World War II, was created by Lawrence Wackett on the basis of experience acquired during the production on license of the North American NA-16 (the multirole two-seater that gave rise to the prolific series of Texan-Harvard trainers in the United States), which was christened Wirraway. Clauses in the contract with North American also allowed for eventual modifications to the basic model, and, driven by the urgency of the situation, CAC's chief designer decided to develop the fighter using the basic structure of this aircraft as a starting point. This proved to be a wise choice: as well as benefitting from the advantages of using an airframe that had already been carefully tested, it meant that most of the existing production infrastructures could be employed. The program was launched on December 21, 1941, and the prototype took to the air on May 29 of the following year. It kept the Wirraway's wings, landing gear and tail fins. However, the rest of the fuselage was entirely new and had been improved to house the large and powerful Pratt & Whitney Twin Wasp radial engine.

Tests revealed the CA-12 Boomerang to be basically without faults, easy to fly and very maneuverable. Production was launched immediately on the basis of an initial order for a first lot amounting to 150 aircraft placed in February 1942. These production series aircraft were delivered to the units from October 10 onward, and following an intensive period of preparation with the pilots, they were consigned to the combat units. On April 4, 1943, the first fighter unit (84th Squadron) was declared operative in New Guinea. Production of the initial series continued until June of the same year, and the Boomerang Mk.I was followed by 95 aircraft belonging to the Mk.II series, which were slightly modified and designated CA-13. The final series included 49 CA-19 Boomerang Mk.IIs, with further improvements, and the last of these was delivered in February 1945.

The total of 250 aircraft also included a single CA-14 built in order to improve the plane's performance at altitude. This aircraft was provided with a supercharged engine and had modified tail planes. However, it never went into production, because the availability of the greatly superior Spitfire Mk.VIII made it unnecessary.

Despite its overall inferiority compared to the powerful and effective Japanese fighters, the Boomerang was used with particular intensity as an interceptor throughout 1943. Toward the end of the following year, the aircraft were gradually withdrawn from this role, following the arrival of the more effective British and American combat planes. The Boomerangs thus passed to the units cooperating with the army and were successfully employed as tactical support planes. They distinguished themselves in missions of this type up to the last day of the war.

---

color plate

Commonwealth CA-13 5th Squadron Royal Australian Air Force - Bougainville, New Guinea 1943

Aircraft:	Commonwealth CA-12
Nation:	Australia
Manufacturer:	Commonwealth Aircraft Corp.
Type:	Fighter
Year:	1942
Engine:	Pratt & Whitney R-1830 S3C 4-G Twin Wasp, 14-cylinder radial, air-cooled, 1,200 hp
Wingspan:	36 ft 1 in (10.97 m)
Length:	25 ft 6 in (7.77 m)
Height:	9 ft 7 in (2.92 m)
Weight:	8,260 lb (3,742 kg)
Maximum speed:	305 mph (491 km/h) at 15,542 ft (4,725 m)
Ceiling:	34,095 ft (10,365 m)
Range:	930 miles (1,500 km)
Armament:	2 × 20 mm cannons; 4 machine guns
Crew:	1

A Boomerang in service with the 5th Squadron of the Royal Australian Air Force.

ITALY

The overall inferiority of the *Regia Aeronautica*, sensationally apparent right from the first year of the war, did not substantially change during the conflict, at least at a quantitative level. However, the sector in which a definite improvement did take place was that of the fighters, thanks to the determining help of Italy's German ally.

In 1940, more than half of the *Regia Aeronautica*'s fighter line was still based on the Fiat C.R.42 biplanes, with the rest consisting of the more advanced, but still inadequate Fiat G.50 and Macchi M.C.200 monoplanes. At the time, the most serious obstacle slowing down the design of a competitive combat plane was the lack of an effective in-line engine. As it was impossible to develop such an engine, both powerful and reliable, in time, it was decided to import the Daimler Benz DB 601 from Germany in order to equip a second generation of fighters.

This engine, with its excellent characteristics, its long operative experience, and its great potential for development, proved to be the ideal choice and made it possible for the Italian aeronautical industry to make the qualitative leap that it was lacking. In several versions, the Daimler Benz eventually equipped all the second and third generation italian fighters. The first examples were the Macchi M.C.202 *Folgore* (considered overall the best of the entire conflict) and the Reggiane Re.2001. Both these aircraft went into service in 1941.

However, the most significant progress came too late. Toward the end of spring 1942 tests began on the three "Series 5" fighters (the Macchi M.C.205 *Veltro*, the Fiat G.55 *Centauro*, and the Reggiane Re.2005), characterized not only by the adoption of the more powerful Daimler Benz DB 605 engine, but also by the overcoming of the inadequacy in armament that, up till then, had affected the efficiency of the *Regia Aeronautica*'s combat planes. However, these three aircraft, which were not only the best of their kind to be built by the Italian aeronautical industry during the war, but were also the first to be truly competitive with those then being produced by Great Britain and the United States, did not have a significant career in the course of operations. In fact, they did not go into service until the spring-summer of 1943, by which time the fate of the nation in the war was practically sealed, and they were manufactured in very small numbers. Lacking raw materials, with its factories plagued by Allied bombing attacks, during the final year of the war Italy could never have been able to maintain the great pace of mass production. On the other hand, the industrial network could never have been able to reach particularly high levels of production, especially when compared with the enormous quantities recorded in Great Britain, Germany and the United States. In 1940, aeronautical production amounted to 3,257 aircraft; the following year this figure had only slightly improved, with an overall total of 3,503 aircraft; in 1942, there was even a drop in production, with 2,818 aircraft of every type being built.

Chronology

1941

May. The 274th Long-Range Bomber Squadron is formed, the first and only unit to be provided with the four-engine Piaggio P.108.

September. The *Regia Aeronautica* orders the first 200 Reggiane Re.2002 *Ariete*, the best fighter-bomber it was to send into combat. Although deliveries began in March 1942, this aircraft did not go into service until it was too late, in March 1943.

1942

April 19. The prototype of the Macchi M.C.205 *Veltro* fighter, the first of the so-called third generation of Italian fighters during the war whose construction was made possible by the availability of the German Daimler Benz DB 605 engine, takes to the air. Just over 300 Macchi M.C.205s were built, and they went into service in the *Regia Aeronautica* in April 1943. After September 8, 1943, approximately 140 of these aircraft constituted the initial nucleus of the fighter units of the *Repubblica Sociale Italiana*, and they had an intensive operative career until the summer of 1944.

April 30. Maiden flight of the Fiat G.55 *Centauro* prototype, the second Italian third generation fighter. Fast, powerful, and competitive with the best of British and American production at the time, this aircraft did not become operative in the *Regia Aeronautica* until June 1943, when thirty or so went into service. A further 150 went into service in the units of the R.S.I., where they fought until the final stages of the war.

May 9. The prototype of the Reggiane Re.2005 *Sagittario*, the last and best combat plane built by Reggiane and the third example of the third generation of Italian fighters, takes to the air. About thirthy were built, despite 750 having been ordered in February 1943. Its operative career in the *Regia Aeronautica* was practically non existent and lasted from May 1943 to the day of the armistice.

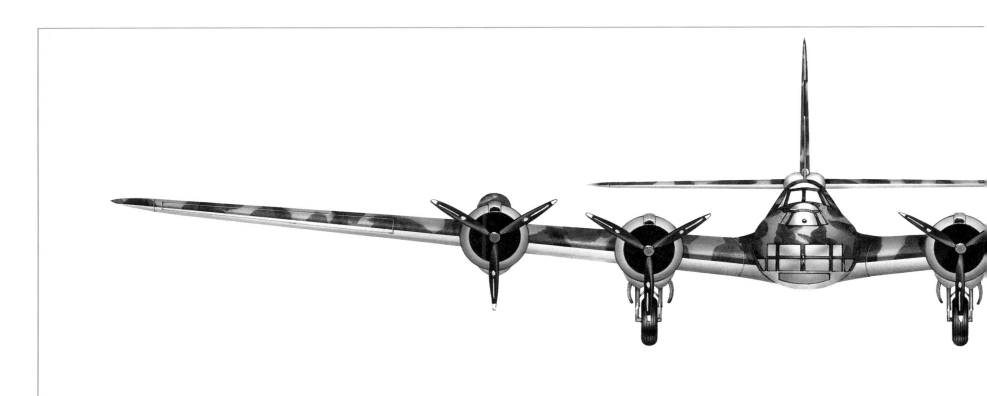

PIAGGIO P.108 B

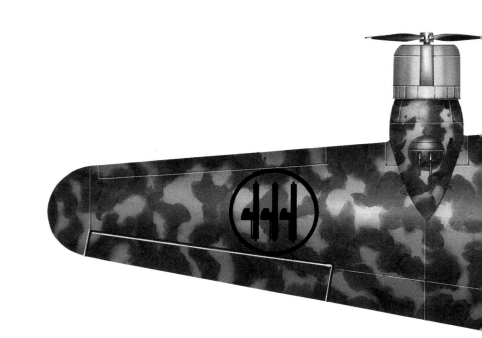

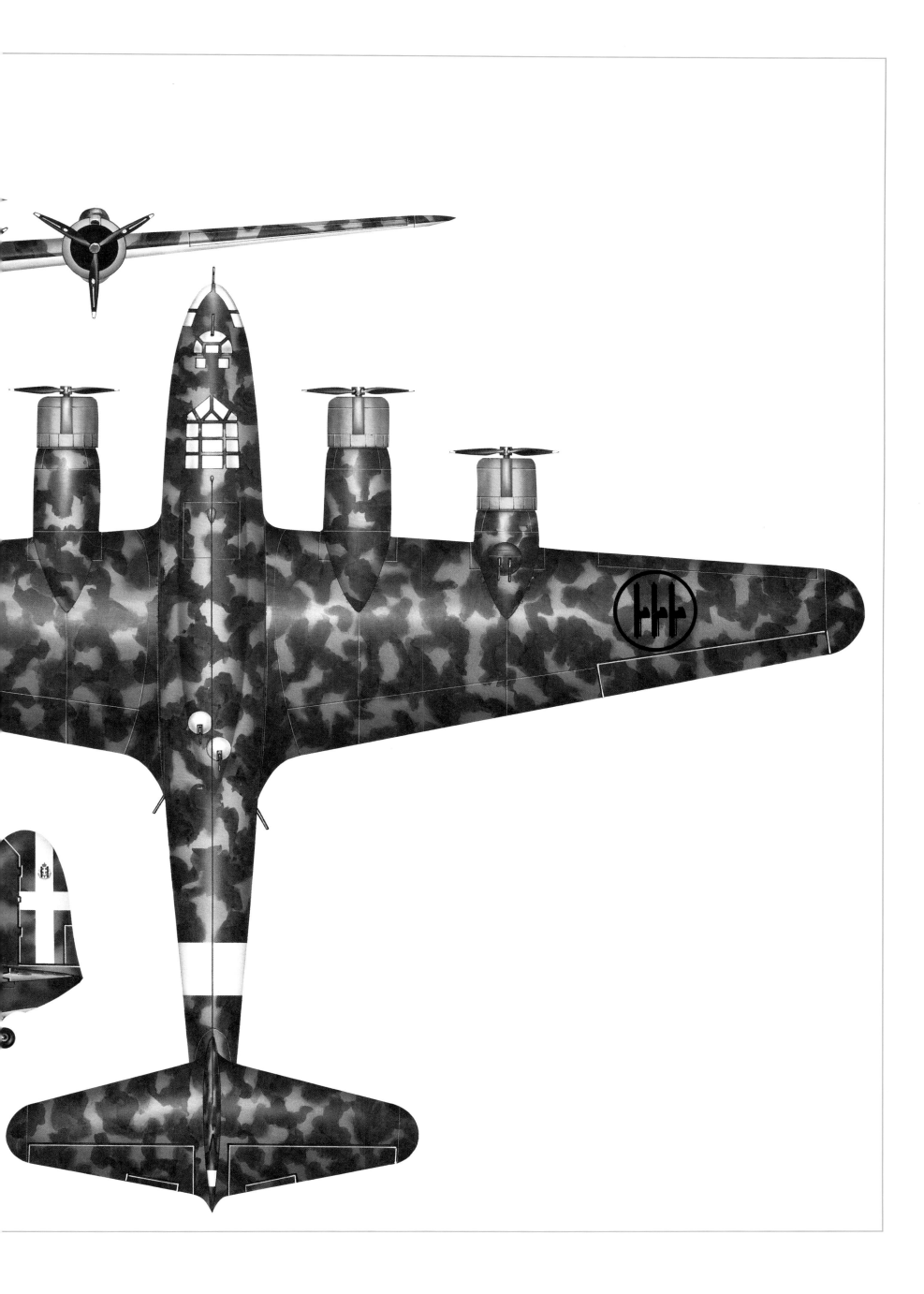

The Piaggio P.108 was the only four-engine heavy bomber employed by the *Regia Aeronautica* during World War II. Although it arrived on the scene too late to play an effective role in the course of operations, from many points of view this aircraft was remarkable compared to the rest of Italian aeronautical production of the period. Its overall performance was excellent, and its combat potential was great, but above all was the advanced nature of its design, which made it competitive with the best aircraft in the world at the time. Only 24 P.108B (bombers) were completed, between November 1939 and August 1943: their operative career started at the beginning of June 1942 and took place mainly in the Mediterranean, although on an irregular basis.

The project was launched in March 1937 by Giovanni Casiraghi, a young engineer called in by Piaggio to replace Giovanni Pegna, the chief designer who had left the company early in 1936. Casiraghi had acquired valuable experience (from November 1927 to February 1936) working in the American aeronautical industry, and this training lay at the basis of his design for a four-engine bomber, already developed by Pegna with the P-50 model. The P.108 slowly took shape, revealing the originality behind its layout and characteristics. It was an all-metal low-wing monoplane with retractable landing gear and was powered by four Piaggio P.XII radial engines generating 1,350 hp each. The defensive armament was particularly effective and consisted of four 12.7 mm machine guns installed in pairs in two radio-controlled turrets in the external engine nacelles, two 7.7 mm weapons situated to the sides of the central part of the fuselage, a 12.7 mm machine gun in a turret in the belly, and a similar weapon in the nose; the offensive armament could reach a maximum of 7,725 lb (3,500 kg) of bombs, all contained inside the fuselage.

The project was presented in the ministerial competition that took place in 1939, in which it came up against a strong rival in the CANT Z.1014, presented by Filippo Zappata. This model was initially judged the winner, although Piaggio eventually succeed-ed in winning the competition by drastically lowering its prices (by 50 percent). The P.108 prototype was completed by October 1939 and took to the air on November 24. A long phase of official evaluations followed, during which the new bomber was prepared definitively. The only unit to be equipped with the P.108B was the 274th Long-Range Bomber Squadron, which was formed at the end of May 1941 with the first production series aircraft. However, operative training proved to be longer than expected, and it was not until June 9, 1942, that the aircraft carried out its first mission, research and bombing of shipping near the Balearic islands. The 274th Squadron was subsequently used in attacks on Gibraltar and Algeria. The P.108B's career came to an end in September 1943, when most of the surviving aircraft fell into the hands of the Germans who, however, did not use them in missions.

Several versions were derived from the basic model. An interesting one was the P.108A (Artillery) for antishipping attack. It began flight testing in March 1943 and was derived from the B but provided with a 102 mm cannon in the nose. In 1942 the prototypes of the P.108C version appeared (this was a civilian version with pressurized cabin for 32 passengers and was destined for service on routes to South America) as well as that of the P.108T (for military transport); both were characterized by a new and larger fuselage. The P.108Ts were the only ones to go into production, with an order for nine aircraft. Almost all of these were captured by the Germans and were used by the transport units of the Luftwaffe, together with the Junkers Ju.290 and the Arado Ar.232. They were widely adopted during the evacuation of Sevastopol and the Crimea from April to May 1944.

color plate

Piaggio P.108B 274th Bomber Squadron *Regia Aeronautica* - Pisa 1941. The aircraft which crashed during landing at Pisa on August 7th, 1941, killing Captain Bruno Mussolini

Aircraft:	Piaggio P.108B
Nation:	Italy
Manufacturer:	S.A. Piaggio & Co.
Type:	Bomber
Year:	1942
Engine:	4 Piaggio P.XII RC 35, 18-cylinder radial, air-cooled, 1,350 hp each
Wingspan:	105 ft 3 in (32.00 m)
Length:	75 ft 4 in (22.92 m)
Height:	25 ft 3 in (7.70 m)
Weight:	59,205 lb (26,820 kg)
Maximum speed:	267 mph (430 km/h) at 13,815 ft (4,200 m)
Ceiling:	19,736 ft (6,000 m)
Range:	2,173 miles (3,500 km)
Armament:	8 machine guns; 7,725 lb (3,500 kg) of bombs
Crew:	6

The Piaggio P.108 *Artigliere*, a bomber transformed for an antishipping role by the installation of a 102 mm cannon in the fuselage.

The first production aircraft of the Piaggio P.108 bomber. The remote-controlled armament is installed on the external engines.

CONTENTS